Methadone Maintenance Treatment

Best Practices in Case Management

Kate Tschakovsky
Chair, Working Advisory Panel

Centre for Addiction and Mental Health
Centre de toxicomanie et de santé mentale

Library and Archives Canada Cataloguing in Publication

Tschakovsky, Kate
    Methadone maintenance treatment : Best practices in case management /
Kate Tschakovsky.

Includes bibliographical references.
Issued also in electronic format.
ISBN 978-0-88868-827-9

    1. Methadone maintenance.   2. Social work with drug addicts.   I. Centre for
Addiction and Mental Health   II. Title.

RC568.M4T83 2009   362.29'37   C2009-901455-6

ISBN: 978-0-88868-827-9 (PRINT)
ISBN: 978-0-88868-828-6 (PDF)
ISBN: 978-0-88868-829-3 (HTML)

Printed in Canada
Copyright © 2009 Centre for Addiction and Mental Health

This publication may be available in other formats. For information about
alternate formats or other CAMH publications, or to place an order, please contact
Sales and Distribution:
Toll-free: 1-800-661-1111
Toronto: 416 595-6059
E-mail: publications@camh.net
Online store: http://store.camh.net
Website: www.camh.net

CAMH acknowledges the financial support of the Government of Ontario. The views
expressed are the views of the author and do not necessarily reflect those of the
Government of Ontario.

Disclaimer: The vignettes that appear in this guide are fictitious scenarios—composites
of representative cases—created for illustrative and educational purposes. There
are many approaches to client care that follow the principles of best practice. These
scenarios illustrate possible approaches but the strategies they demonstrate should
not be viewed as the only possible or even recommended ones for use in the circumstances described. Workers should abide by their agency's guidelines and professional
requirements, and should seek input from supervisors for challenging situations.

This book was produced by:
Development: Lynn Schellenberg
Editorial: Elizabeth d'Anjou, Mariko Obokata
Design: Nancy Leung, CAMH
Print production: Chris Harris, CAMH
Typesetting: TC Communications Express

4016/ 03-2009 / PZ169

CONTENTS

MEMBERS OF THE WORKING ADVISORY PANEL

Kate Tschakovsky, MSW, RSW, Project Co-ordinator, OpiATE Project, CAMH (Panel Chair)

Cindy DeSousa, BSW, RSW, Therapist, Addiction Medicine Services, CAMH, Toronto

Katia Gouveia, MSW, RSW, Addiction Therapist, Addiction Medicine Services, CAMH, Toronto

Jean-François H.B. Martinbault, BSW, MPM, Acu-Detox Specialist, Methadone Case Manager, Oasis Program, Sandy Hill Community Health Centre, Ottawa

Vonda Mazarakis, CACII Case Manager, Methadone Services, Drouillard Road Clinic, Windsor

Sharon Mulligan, BScN, ICADC, Counsellor, Algoma Health Unit, Community Alcohol/Drug Assessment Program, Algoma District

Patrick Shaw, Methadone Case Manager, Counsellor, The Works, Toronto Public Health

Abi Sprakes, MSW, RSW, PhD (candidate), Manager of Programs & Services, Thunder Bay Counselling Centre

Research assistance

Research assistance was provided to the Working Advisory Panel by Ava Rubin, BA, BEd, Research Co-ordinator, Education Services, CAMH.

ACKNOWLEDGMENTS

Methadone Training Advisory Committee, CAMH
The following committee members regularly contributed their professional perspective and knowledge to the panel and author, by reviewing data and consulting on issues related to methadone maintenance treatment.

Betty Dondertman, Chair
Manager, Education Services, CAMH

Branka Agic, MD, MHSc
Community Health and Education Specialist, Education Services, CAMH

Carol Batstone, RN
Nurse, Addiction Medicine Services, CAMH

Wade Hillier
Manager, Government Programs, College of Physicians and Surgeons of Ontario

Pearl Isaac, RPh, BScPhm
Pharmacist, Pharmacy Department, CAMH

Eva Janecek-Rucker, RPh, BScPhm
Pharmacist, Pharmacy Department, CAMH

Anne Kalvik, RPh, BScPhm
Pharmacist, Pharmacy Department, CAMH

Agnes Kwasnicka, MSc, MD, CCFP
Staff physician, Addiction Medicine Services, CAMH

Lisa Lefebvre, MDCM, CCFP
Addiction Medicine Consultant, Addictions Program, CAMH

Peter Selby, MBBS, CCFP, MHSc, FASAM
Clinical Director, Addictions Program, CAMH
Associate Professor, Departments of Family and Community Medicine,
Psychiatry and Dalla Lana School of Public Health, University of Toronto

Connie Speirs, RN
Nurse, Addiction Medicine Services, CAMH

Beth Sproule, RPh, BScPhm, PharmD
Advanced Practice Pharmacist / Clinician Scientist, Pharmaceutical Services
Department, CAMH

Carol Strike, PhD
Senior Scientist, Health Systems Research and Consulting Unit, CAMH

Other advisers
Mark Erdelyan, MEd, Program Consultant, Policy Education and Health
Promotion, CAMH, Windsor, provided an educational lecture to the panel and
helped with client interviews.

Jenny Oey Cheung, RN, Research Unit, Registered Nurses' Association
of Ontario, provided the panel with information and resources on the
development of best practice guides and the AGREE instrument.

Andrew Johnson, Publication Developer, CAMH, provided the panel with help
and guidance during the document's early stages.

Stakeholder reviewers
The Working Advisory Panel members wish to thank the many reviewers who
took time away from their busy schedules to read and provide feedback about
this document. We greatly appreciate their commitment to the improvement
of case management services. The panel particularly wishes to thank the clients
who participated in the review process but who requested that they not be
named for reasons of confidentiality.

Nicole Balan, Ontario College of Pharmacists

Kim Bray, Addiction Counsellor and Methadone Case Manager, Simcoe
Outreach Services, Barrie

Kate Doornward, Case Manager, Thunder Bay

Morris Field, Community Member

Debra Maki, RN, Team Leader, Case Manager, Lakeview Clinic

Norma Medulun, Regional Director Addiction Programs, Niagara Health System, and President, Addictions Ontario

Lori Naylor, Addiction Therapist, Breakaway Satellite Opiate Addiction Treatment Clinic

Carolyn Plater, BA Hons, MSW Candidate, Lead Clinical Case Manager, Ontario Addiction Treatment Centres

Christopher Sankey, MD

Kelly Sexsmith, Methadone Case Manager/Counsellor, Street Health Centre, Kingston

Shawna Thomas, BSc, Counsellor

Pamela VanBelle, Registered Nurses' Association of Ontario

Christine Werbski, Therapist, Addiction Medicine Services, CAMH

FOREWORD

In our lives, every one of us experiences times when we struggle with a problem or crisis and need help. Often, the struggle to figure out where to get the appropriate help makes our lives even more difficult and can complicate the problem.

When people are faced with the challenge of dependence on drugs that alters their ability to think clearly or even to manage basic daily functions, the additional tasks associated with finding help can be daunting. Providing support for these tasks—the essence of case management—is often an important part of a successful recovery.

This book is important because it guides those whose job it is to help others get the help they need. It is the first evidence-based guide written specifically for case managers working in methadone maintenance treatment in Ontario.

The role of a methadone case manager is complex, requiring skills in counselling and communication; a large body of knowledge about drug use, health and social problems; and knowledge about the many potential agencies and organizations for referral.

This guide is therefore a valuable tool, both for case managers and for the organizations that employ them. In the course of recommending best practice guidelines, it provides an opportunity for case managers to reflect upon how they might enhance the way they interact with their clients. The scenarios, practice points and practice perspectives could be used to stimulate discussion in staff meetings. For organizations, the description of the core of knowledge required can both facilitate hiring the appropriate staff and provide a framework for a training plan for existing staff. And although its recommendations are about case management best practices in methadone maintenance treatment programs specifically, the guide's practical focus also makes it useful and interesting to other case managers working in addictions or mental health.

This book may also assist planners and funders in addressing opioid addiction and methadone treatment with a comprehensive, client-centred perspective within a co-ordinated system approach. It speaks to the importance of addressing our knowledge and attitudes about the people who need support—and to the kinds of support they want.

The guide includes the voices of the people who are best able to describe the services that will help them stabilize their lives. These voices evaluate the services they receive and tell us first-hand the importance of providing accessible service and support.

Opioid addiction is on the rise (in Ontario, the majority of people who use opioids are using prescription medications), and methadone maintenance is a medically recognized treatment for it. Many of those who take methadone state clearly that case management is an essential service that complements their medical treatment. Readers of this book will learn just how case management helps people achieve stability and health in their lives.

Christine Bois
OpiATE Project Manager
CAMH, Ottawa

SECTION I: BACKGROUND

About this guide

Audience

This guide is intended first and foremost for case managers who provide direct service to clients in methadone maintenance treatment (MMT), but also for the other members of the teams who care for and provide services to these clients—doctors, nurses, pharmacists, managers, administrators and support staff—and for students and educators in programs relating to case management.

Several other categories of reader also exist for this document. Perhaps the largest of these is the staff and management of health and social support services that work with MMT clients. These services are numerous and varied and include:
- financial support programs (such as Ontario Works and the Ontario Disability Support Program)
- shelters
- housing agencies
- hospital emergency rooms
- mental health crisis services
- other mental health services
- child protection agencies
- criminal justice services
- vocational and education programs
- addiction treatment programs that are not MMT specific
- needle exchange programs
- street outreach programs.

As the co-ordinating hub at the centre of care surrounding MMT clients, the case manager has a perspective that is by necessity holistic. Learning more about MMT from the case manager's perspective may help social service providers to view their own interactions with MMT clients differently, with an increased understanding of the impact that their decisions about clients' lives—especially decisions that reduce a service's accessibility— have on clients' treatment outcomes and overall well-being.

For the same reasons, policy and regulatory bodies that have direct input into how methadone services are delivered and that support these practices at the treatment system level are also an important part of the audience for the recommendations and supporting information in this guide.

Finally, this guide is also intended for clients, both as individuals and as collective consumer and self-advocacy groups. Because MMT services and how they are delivered vary from community to community, it can be challenging for clients to determine just what kind of care they are getting and how it compares to optimal models of care. It has been well established in general health care and mental health care that treatment outcomes improve when the client is a partner in his or her treatment and is well informed and able to identify and advocate for standards of service. It is reasonable to extrapolate that the same holds true in MMT. For this purpose, this guide thus complements a range of information from CAMH specifically written for clients about MMT, in particular *Methadone Maintenance Treatment: Client Handbook* (CAMH, 2008).

Content

Section I of this guide contains background information, beginning with this discussion of the guide's audience, content and uses. This section also describes the guide's scope and purpose and the process of its development. Section I also includes a discussion of the context of MMT case management in Ontario, with a particular focus on treatment philosophies.

The best practice recommendations in Section II form the heart of this guide. The recommendations are presented first in summary form, then in more detail, accompanied by text that discusses, supports, amplifies and explains them.

Section II also contains the following features, designed to add information or illustrate possible application of the recommendations in actual practice:

- **practice points** that give direct, practical advice for case managers on ways to put the recommendations into action
- **fictional cases** that present reflections on and responses to different case management scenarios
- **information boxes** that provide definitions or additional background, or flag issues important to case managers
- **client consultation findings** that provide clients' perspectives on issues in MMT case management (see "The development process" for more information on the client consultation)
- **client quotes**, obtained during the client consultation phase of this guide's development, that share the clients' experiences and their thoughts about what case managers are doing well or should be doing differently to best help them

Section III, "Beyond the recommendations," begins with a list of research gaps identified by the panel members during the course of their work on the guide. This section includes a set of implementation strategies, with the understanding that the applicability of individual strategies will vary among programs and service providers according to their circumstances, resources and focus. Section III also presents a framework with which to monitor and evaluate the effect of these guidelines over time, and a discussion of a plan for periodic review and updating of this guide. A list of references concludes the section.

Appendix A offers a brief overview of related and emerging issues; Appendix B is a selected resources list.

Finally, a note on what is *not* in this guide: This document is not intended to be a comprehensive primer on MMT. It assumes the reader has basic knowledge about the use of methadone in the treatment of opioid dependence.

Uses

The guide can be used in a number of ways:

- Managers and staff members of programs and services can review how they currently deliver services and identify what changes they need to make to become more aligned with best practice.
- Clinicians and clinical supervisors can use the case scenarios to reflect on their own practice.
- Physicians and pharmacists can use the recommendations and supporting information to reflect on their understanding of case management in MMT and to improve the ways they work with case management services.
- Providers of community health and social services can use the guide to think about additional ways to make their services more accessible to MMT clients.
- Research and scientific groups can use the section that identifies current gaps in research and knowledge about MMT in Ontario, particularly around program delivery structures and corresponding outcome measures, as a guide to areas of future study.
- Clients and client advocacy groups can use the guide to identify what MMT services should look like, and compare this with the actual services they are receiving. Advocacy for improved services can be based on the recommendations.
- Educators in social work, nursing and counselling programs can use this guide to ensure that educational programs reflect best practice in case management of MMT.
- Professional regulatory bodies (such as the Ontario College of Social Work and Social Service Work and the Ontario College of Nurses) can use the guide to further their understanding of the core competencies for case management in MMT and to incorporate this understanding into the training, licensing and evaluation of their members.
- Programs that provide services to MMT clients can identify the additional supports (such as greater staff resources, improved education or more extensive data collection) that will help them to incorporate best practices into their work.
- The Ontario Ministry of Health and Long-Term Care and the province's Local Health Integration Networks can use this guide to understand more about the role of case management in MMT and to inform decisions about increased or ongoing funding.

Responsibility for development

Origins: The OpiATE Project

One of the recommendations of the report of the Methadone Maintenance Treatment Practices Task Force (2007) was that the Centre for Addiction and Mental Health "lead the development of standards and guidelines for addiction counsellors, with a particular emphasis on methadone maintenance treatment." The report also recommended that CAMH, "in consultation with the Canadian Society of Addiction Medicine and others, continue to develop and offer educational courses in addictions in partnership with schools of medicine, nursing, pharmacy, psychology and social work in Ontario. . . . "

Soon after this report's publication, and with funding from the Government of Ontario, CAMH embarked on the OpiATE Project. The project had three main objectives:

1. To develop sustainable biopsychosocial treatment models for people with opioid dependence by engaging communities to increase awareness of the benefits of treatment for opioid dependence
2. To raise awareness about issues related to opioid dependence and reduce stigma and marginalization of addiction clients
3. To expand training and professional supports, including the development of a certificate program in opioid addiction for nurses, physicians, pharmacists, case managers and counsellors

As part of the OpiATE Project, the case management best practices guide was developed by a panel of case managers and other professionals convened by CAMH. This work was conducted independent of any bias or influence from the Government of Ontario.

The Working Advisory Panel

The development of this guide officially began in March 2008 with the appointment of the project author and chair of the Working Advisory Panel (Kate Tschakovsky). In May 2008, the chair began recruitment of the panel, inviting experienced case managers who worked directly with MMT clients at agencies funded by the Ontario Ministry of Health and Long-Term Care.* The factors considered in the composition of the panel are shown in Table 1.

To avoid having any one region overrepresented, the number of advisory panel members from Toronto was restricted to the equivalent of two dedicated members (one "full-time" panel member and two who shared the position on a rotating basis). Care was taken to include a variety of agency types—small clinics, hospital-based clinics, offsite case management centres and community health centres—as well as representation from communities identified by the OpiATE project as "high need": Ottawa, Thunder Bay, Chatham-Kent and Halton.

There were no strict educational requirements, though panel members with at least two years of direct clinical experience were sought out. The intent was that the panel of case managers represent the wide variety of professional backgrounds, training and available resources that exist among their colleagues across Ontario.

Membership applications were reviewed by the chair and an adviser (CAMH Community Health and Education Specialist Branka Agic). The final panel consisted of the chair and seven panel members. All members had extensive experience with providing MMT case management services.

---

* The panel wished to include case managers from non-LHIN-funded agencies but was not able to do so. It is the panel's hope that future editions of this guide may include their representation so as to present a more complete picture of MMT case management services offered within the province.

TABLE 1

**Factors considered in composition of the
Working Advisory Panel**

- Geographic region

- Type of agency and service

- Permission from manager to participate

- Time commitment to work on project

- Experience with MMT and service delivery (minimum 2 years)

- Expressed interest in the project

- Willingness to work with others having different perspectives and experience

Scope and purpose

Objectives

The Working Advisory Panel began its development of this guide with the following objectives:

- to identify essential knowledge, clinical skills and practice approaches that optimize and support case management of MMT
- to identify program philosophy, value base, orientation and service delivery approaches that support case management in MMT
- to identify the ways in which external health services and social support systems, as well as policy and regulatory bodies, can support case management of MMT
- to identify where further research and data are needed in order to improve best practice

Setting the parameters

CLIENT POPULATION

We decided to focus on clients currently in methadone treatment but also to include a brief overview of clients who exit treatment early, as our investigation into the literature indicated that it had some significant and conclusive things to say about the role of case management for these groups.

TYPES OF METHADONE TREATMENT

We explored what we meant by the term "methadone treatment," deciding to exclude from our investigation specific rapid, time-limited tapering treatments and methadone treatment prescribed only to treat pain.

GEOGRAPHIC REGION AND TREATMENT SETTINGS

Our focus was on issues relevant to Ontario, though the existing research was often broad and general and not specifically focused on Ontario issues. We decided to view research from around the world, but always to evaluate it in terms of its relevancy to Ontario settings, to discuss the limits to its applicability and to identify gaps in the research. We decided to be as inclusive of the various regions and settings (Northern, rural, urban, mid-size communities) as possible and to examine the issues and concerns unique to each of these areas.

Clinical questions

With objectives and parameters established, the panel formulated the following clinical questions:

1. What must case managers or case management agencies know and do to help their clients achieve the best possible outcomes with MMT?
2. What must physicians know and do to support best practice in case management?
3. What must pharmacists know and do to support best practice in case management?
4. What must programs do and what systems must be in place to support best practice in case management?
5. What do other health and support services need to do to support best practice in case management?
6. What do policy-makers and regulatory bodies need to know and do to support best practice in case management?
7. What data needs to be collected on an ongoing basis to help support best practice in case management?

8. What kind of future research will support and inform best practices in case management?
9. What kind of evaluation and monitoring of methadone treatment will support and inform best practice in case management?

The panel then began the development process for the guide.

The development process

The advisory panel met regularly during a six-month period (June through November 2008). Its early communications, to identify topics and areas of consideration for the guide and to formulate the scope and clinical questions, were by e-mail. In August, research and data extraction began, and the panel began meeting weekly via teleconference using an online file-sharing portal; a one-day face-to-face meeting was held September 16 at CAMH. The panel reviewed all relevant research and citations through the data extraction templates, reviewed drafts and provided feedback on the recommendations as they evolved. The panel also assisted with the design of the client consultation questionnaire.

Group decision making about content and focus followed a consensus model, with consultation from a senior research adviser (Carol Strike) on challenging issues.

Literature search

Having discussed possible content areas to explore and having formulated the clinical questions, the panel identified keywords and phrases to use in the literature search (see Table 2).

A search using these keywords in the databases listed in Table 3 yielded 457 articles, reports and studies. From these, the panel excluded
- items not published in the English language
- items not published within the last 20 years, apart from a few seminal studies
- materials that, while they contained the keywords and phrases, did not contain substantive discussion that was directly applicable to or could be extrapolated to address the clinical questions.

All research for the project was gathered by Working Advisory Panel Chair Kate Tschakovsky and by Ava Rubin, Research Co-ordinator, Education Services, CAMH, with the assistance of CAMH library staff.

TABLE 2

Keywords and phrases used in database search

- addictions counselling
- best practice for pharmacists in MMT
- best practices in case management
- best practices in counselling
- case management
- case management accreditation
- case management in addictions
- case management in MMT
- case management with hepatitis C
- case management with HIV
- concurrent disorders in MMT
- counselling accreditation
- counselling in MMT
- diversity in addictions counselling
- ethics in case management
- ethics in counselling
- ethnicity in addictions counselling
- harm reduction counselling
- impact of case management in MMT
- interdisciplinary collaboration in health care
- interprofessional collaboration in health care
- legal issues in case management
- MMT employment issues
- MMT treatment best practice
- remote technology and counselling
- role of case management in MMT
- substance use and mental health treatment
- women and substance use counselling

TABLE 3
Databases searched

- Australian Department of Health and Ageing
- CAMH database
- CANBASE
- CCSA DOCS (Canadian Centre for Substance Abuse)
- CINAHL (Cumulative Index to Nursing and Allied Health Literature)
- CSAT (Center for Substance Abuse Treatment)
- EMBASE
- Euro-*Meth*work
- HealthSTAR
- ISDD (Institute for the Study of Drug Dependence) Britain
- Medline
- National Guideline Clearinghouse
- NIDA (National Institute on Drug Abuse)
- University of British Columbia database
- University of Toronto database

Research evaluation

All sources were reviewed and data extracted in the form of a summary. Research studies, systematic reviews and guideline documents were evaluated and scored.

The data from the remaining 129 articles were extracted and summarized according to the following criteria:
- citation source (reputable journal or other reputable source)
- conflict of interest declared
- major theme or construct
- research approach
- research design
- major findings and conclusions
- recommendations for further research
- limitations and considerations

Each article was also ranked according to the design and strength of the study, and the level of its applicability to Ontario contexts was noted.

Quantitative, qualitative and systematic reviews and advisory papers and best practice guides on related topics (for example, best practices for mental health care) were included. They were evaluated according to their scope, presentation of evidence, level of expertise, stakeholder involvement and clarity of recommendations or conclusions.

The data were compiled in extraction tables organized according to themes. This material was made available to the Working Advisory Panel to read and review as recommendations were formulated.

To ensure that its development process and recommendations were sound, the panel self-assessed its methodology using the AGREE instrument.*

Client consultation

Conducting a client consultation was an additional and important part of the panel's investigation. Clients were invited to provide information about their experience with case management during their MMT, as well as to give their feedback, through a brief, questionnaire-based interview, on what worked well in the case management relationship and what changes they would like to see. The interviews were conducted in person by project staff who were not involved in providing direct case management services and who did not work for the agencies whose clients were consulted. Clients were interviewed in all four of the high-need communities identified at the project outset; as well, there was a small pilot group in Toronto.

We visited 12 different methadone programs and providers in seven communities and asked for client volunteers to speak with us about their experiences with MMT. Staff then conducted interviews with 30 women

---

* AGREE Collaboration. (2001). Appraisal of Guidelines for Research & Evaluation (AGREE) Instrument. Available: www.agreecollaboration.org/.

and 39 men, who ranged in age from 19 to 60. The majority of the women were in the 21-to-30-year-old category and the majority of men were in the 31-to-40-year-old category.

All of the clients consulted were undergoing MMT at the time of their interviews. Most had been on methadone for either less than two years (the largest percentage of clients interviewed) or for more than five years (the second-largest percentage of those interviewed). The majority of the clients consulted received their treatment at clinics that had multiple services onsite, such as urine drug screening, case management and nursing.

Interviews were one on one, lasted about 25 minutes and used a combination of structured and open-ended questions. Clients were paid $20 for their time.

This consultation was not a research trial, and its application to the general population of MMT clients in Ontario is limited. It does, however, provide a record of some client concerns and thoughts regarding their experiences with case management in MMT. Their responses contribute an important perspective and an immediacy to this guide on the subject of best practice, through quotations from the interviews and questionnaire findings presented alongside the recommendations and discussion in Section II.*

Formulation of recommendations

Having identified potential topic areas through its clinical questions, the Working Advisory Panel reviewed the available evidence relating to these topics. The data extraction was used to facilitate discussion and highlight the gaps in the research (results that were either inconclusive or not relevant in an Ontario-focused context).

These gaps in the research and an imperfect fit between evidence and the clinical questions introduced additional challenges for the panel

---

* More detailed information on this consultation, including an explanation of the data-gathering tools used and a complete list of the findings, is contained in an unpublished document. Interested readers may request a copy by contacting CAMH Publication Services.

in its evaluation of the research and formulation of recommendations. For example, the research does not agree on what exactly case managers do, what their background and training should be, and how their contribution to methadone maintenance treatment can be measured and evaluated. Some studies examined a particular function or objective of the case manager role, such as therapeutic engagement or reduction of early treatment exit; others looked at the often-conflicting demands case managers try to meet: providing the support that clients say they value while operating under the time and resource constraints of the agencies and social systems within which they must work.

As well, the data that has been collected or published on case management in MMT is of varying evidence levels, with few level I or II studies. It is not surprising, therefore, that much of the available research did not focus specifically on issues unique to case management in MMT practice, or to the different circumstances in which case managers work in Ontario. In these instances, the panel members used their experience and insight as clinicians and MMT service providers to extrapolate from the evidence.

The panel drafted its recommendations, identifying and describing the practices and approaches that constitute best practice in case management in MMT within the specific context of Ontario, based on a synthesis of the available published research and the expert knowledge of the panel members.

Each recommendation was assigned a classification indicating the level of evidence supporting it. The level codes are described in Table 4.

The panel also made note of areas where there were gaps in the existing research; its recommendations for future studies are included in Section III, "Research gaps."

TABLE 4
Classification of recommendations: Levels of evidence

Ia   Evidence obtained from meta-analysis or systematic review of randomized control trials

Ib   Evidence obtained from at least one randomized control trial

IIa   Evidence obtained from at least one well-designed, controlled study without randomization

IIb   Evidence obtained from at least one other type of well-designed, quasi-experimental study without randomization

III   Evidence obtained from well-designed, non-experimental descriptive studies, such as comparative studies, co-relational studies and case studies

IV   Evidence obtained from expert committees, reports, opinions and/or clinical experiences of respected authorities

Stakeholder review

The draft guide underwent review by members of the panel, members of the Methadone Maintenance Treatment Initiatives Steering Committee of the Ministry of Health and Long-Term Care, CAMH staff and a number of other stakeholders, including clinicians from various professions involved in MMT and clients. (The reviewers are listed in the Acknowledgments.)

Feedback from the reviews was used to improve and clarify the content of the guide.

Definitions

Case management, counselling

Much of the literature reviewed for this guide used these terms loosely and interchangeably. There were many additional terms used—key worker, program worker, counsellor, case worker, outreach worker and treatment co-ordinator—to describe various functions and the people who performed them.

The Ontario Ministry of Health and Long-Term Care uses the term "case manager" to identify the area of practice toward which this guide is targeted. For the purposes of this guide, we will refer to the function as "case management" and the people who perform that function as "case managers." As yet, there are no credentials that can be earned or professional standards one must meet to be a case manager, in contrast with, for example, the professions of nurse, pharmacist and social worker. People with a wide variety of educational backgrounds perform case management functions.

Similarly, the term "counsellor" is vaguely defined. There is no distinct profession of counsellor but rather a variety of qualifications that allow people to perform a counselling function. "Counselling" is one of the functions performed by case managers.

Client, patient, consumer

In the literature, depending on the audience for which it is written, the terms "client," "patient" and "consumer" are variously used to describe the person at the receiving end of health care services. The word "client" is most commonly used in case management practice, so this guide adheres to that usage, regardless of the term used in the study or research cited.

Opiate, opioid

Opioids are drugs that bind to opioid receptors. Opiates are a subclass of these drugs that are derived from opium, whereas other opioids are synthetic or semi-synthetic opium-like drugs. The discussions of treatment and dependence in this guide include all opioid drugs, not just opiates, and therefore use the term "opioids."

Refractory

Research uses many different terms to describe clients who continue to use opioids despite receiving comprehensive treatment and adequate doses of methadone. Such terms include "treatment resistant," "high need–high risk" and "hard to serve" or "relapse prone" to describe these clients. In this guide, we have used the terms "refractory" and "chronically relapsing" to describe clients who are not able to sustain consistent behavioural changes and reduced drug use. We emphasize that these terms are not intended to blame clients for these behaviours; many factors, such as the treatment received, the socioeconomic or psychological environment and co-existing physical or psychological conditions can contribute to the complexities of clients who don't respond well to treatment. A client's poor outcome may have as much to do with poor treatment fit as with his or her behaviour.

MMT case management in Ontario

I urged that physicians should see that the problem was one of rehabilitating people with a very complicated mixture of social problems on top of a specific medical problem, and that they ought to tailor their programs to the kinds of problems they were dealing with. The strength of the early programs as designed by Marie Nyswander was in their sensitivity to individual human problems. The stupidity of thinking that just giving methadone will solve a complicated social problem seems to me beyond comprehension.

—Vincent Dole, 1982 (quoted in Courtwright, 1989)

Methadone treatment has been available in Ontario for close to 40 years. The guidelines for its prescription and administration, as well as for service delivery models, have evolved over the years, and so too have the philosophies and approaches on which methadone maintenance treatment (MMT) is based. At one time, treatment with methadone was available only in a few large urban centres, operating from an abstinence orientation; a client's continued substance use often meant discharge from treatment. Today, while greater access is still needed, MMT across all parts of Ontario is the result of an increased understanding over the years of the benefits of a harm-reduction approach in addiction treatment, the importance of treatment retention and engagement, the relationship between injection drug use and the public health issues of HIV and hepatitis C, and the social costs of untreated opioid use.

The value of case management

Case Management Services: a process which includes the designation of a primary worker whose responsibilities include the ongoing assessment of the client and his/her problems, ongoing adjustment of the treatment plan, linking to and coordination of required services, monitoring and support, developing and implementing the discharge plan, and advocating for the client. Case management services are offered regardless where the individual is in the system.
—Ontario Addiction Services Advisory Council, 2000

With this definition, the Ministry of Health and Long-Term Care recognized case management as a category of primary service within addiction treatment. Within the subspecialty of MMT case management, research has strongly identified case management and counselling as essential components of MMT (Australian Department of Health and Ageing, 2003; Collège des médecins du Québec & Ordre des pharmaciens du Québec, 2000; Currie, 2001; Farrell et al., 1996; McCann et al., 1994; NIDA, 1999a). Including these services in the delivery of MMT improves treatment outcomes; specifically, it enhances treatment retention, decreases the use of illegal opioids and other substances and improves overall functioning in the areas of criminality, homelessness, mental health and vocational and educational involvement.

MMT programs that include some form of case management and counselling show superior results to those that provide methadone as a stand-alone intervention (Ball & Ross, 1991; Health Canada, 2002a; Bell, 1998; Leshner, 1999; Gossop, Stewart et al., 2006; Warj et al., 1992; Laken & Ager, 1996; Kay & Peters, 1992).

Access to case management

Despite the fact that the value of case management in MMT is widely acknowledged, programs vary widely in how well they integrate or make available to their clients the essential components of counselling and the other functions of case management. Some methadone clients can easily access case management and counselling because these services are built seamlessly into their treatment programs. Others, for example, those who are treated in smaller communities or through office-based practices, can access methadone to treat their dependence on opioid drugs, but may have little or no access to counselling or other case management supports.

Case managers and counsellors working in the field are also faced with a variety of situations and working environments. Some work in resource-rich communities and programs that value case management and counselling and support their integration into MMT, and where evidence-based practice and program policies and cohesive team approaches to care are the norm. Others find themselves working in isolation from the prescribers and dispensers of methadone in resource-poor communities or in a health or social service program that is unwelcoming to methadone clients and misinformed about MMT, with many barriers to the provision of services to methadone clients.

This guide acknowledges these realities and aims to provide information that will allow case managers working in direct practice to provide the best care for their clients. It also seeks to address issues of program policy and other services because these affect many components of MMT care that fall under the broad description of case management and are essential for the support of best practices in methadone treatment.

Program approaches and treatment matching

How and why clinical and operational decisions are made in an MMT program is influenced by the underlying philosophy, or approach, of the program. Data have not been collected on the prevalence of different philosophies and orientations of MMT programs in Ontario, but anecdotal evidence suggests that they span a wide range.

At one end of the spectrum are very low threshold programs that focus on harm reduction. The aim of such programs is to engage chronically relapsing and complex clients and to continue to provide them with methadone and access to other services despite their ongoing use of opioids or other drugs or their unstable behaviour. At the other end of the spectrum are programs that require clients to be abstinent or mostly abstinent from opioids and other substances and to maintain social stability in terms of employment or school pursuits, and that regard clients' continued use or unstable behaviours as grounds for discharge from the program or transfer to another program. In between are programs that take a moderate approach and are able to accommodate clients who cycle in and out of stability or show only moderate reduction in their use of substances.

In communities where there are choices in treatment approach and treatment matching is possible, a client can find a program that most closely meets his or her needs. However, in communities where there are fewer choices, or no choices, receiving MMT in a program that is more rigid or with an approach other than a harm-reduction one may not be the optimal treatment for less stable or refractory clients.

Evidence shows abstinence-only programs are not as effective as programs that allow for voluntary reduction in drug use without threat of program discharge. Many MMT clients are not served well by abstinence-based programs, and more refractory clients will drop out of such programs and experience greater risk. Harms to the community and public health (such as criminality, HIV infection) are greatly reduced when a harm reduction approach to MMT is used (Platt et al., 1998; Rosenbaum, 1997). The panel's opinion is that having different program models available and consequently being able to provide clients with options in terms of the degree to which abstinence is required for continuance in MMT may be helpful in retaining clients.

Harm reduction and low-threshold MMT programs that provide basic services to marginalized and difficult-to-engage clients show promising results in terms of reducing high-risk behaviours such as injecting, needle sharing, unsafe sex and criminality (Johnson et al., 2001; Csete, 2007; BC MOH, 2005; Phillips & Rosenberg, 2008).

Low-threshold programs are a way of delivering methadone maintenance treatment while at the same time reducing or eliminating many of the elements of more "traditional" methadone programs. The program model is designed for clients who are generally difficult to engage, are not able to comply or uncomfortable complying with the many demands and "rules" of regular methadone maintenance treatment and are at risk for dropping out of treatment altogether.

Characteristics of low-threshold programs include:
- typically shorter waiting times for admission to the program
- no regular collection of urine samples (except as part of the admission and medical screening process)
- no provision for take-home doses
- optional access to case management services (i.e., clients are not mandated for appointments)
- onsite access to harm reduction supplies for injection, inhalation and safer sex.

Clients are required to see a physician for dose adjustment and monitoring but missing appointments or cycling in and out of treatment is not viewed as grounds for dismissal or transfer from the program. The core of low-threshold programs is that they make it easy for clients who are somewhat chaotic and unstable and not a good fit for more traditional programs but who would benefit from methadone maintenance to get the treatment they need (less hassle, easy access service).

Clients can opt to move on to more structured programs if they wish to work toward take-home doses, for example; low-threshold programs, while they generally have no time limit, are often a stepping stone to more traditional forms of MMT.

Contingency management is another therapeutic tool used in many programs. It involves increasing the portion of methadone doses that a client can take at home as he or she provides substance-free results in urine drug screening, and a decrease in take-home doses based on substance-positive results and/or other indicators of instability, such as frequently missed appointments, failure to provide required urine screens or behavioural problems while on clinic or pharmacy premises. Contingency management has been associated with greater treatment retention and decreased substance use, but only if it is based on non-punitive principles and works to effectively engage participants (Rhodes et al., 2003; Sindelar et al., 2007; Bickel et al., 2008; Wood et al., 2006).

Summary

MMT clients are best served by a harm reduction approach; refractory clients may especially benefit from low-threshold programs. Contingency management is an effective therapeutic tool, but only if it is non-punitive, if the principles are thoroughly explained to clients and if it contributes positively to treatment engagement.

In Ontario, it is not known to what extent various MMT programs and providers practise from a low-threshold or harm reduction model and what types of contingency management strategies are used. Case managers may be aware of a particular program's or prescriber's approach and may try to match clients to a program with an approach best suited to the client, but this can be challenging in communities with few treatment resources because of wait-lists, travel and the geographic admission boundaries of some programs.

SECTION II: RECOMMENDATIONS AND DISCUSSION

Summary of recommendations

The recommendations throughout this guide are ranked by the level of evidence that supports them. The levels are described in Section I, "Formulation of recommendations." Please see Table 4, page 21 for more information. The list of clinical questions that these recommendations address can be found on pages 12 to 13.

The role of case management in MMT

These recommendations address clinical questions 1 to 6. Recommendations 1 to 4 are directed to case managers and the agencies they work for, and to other members of the methadone maintenance treatment (MMT) team. Recommendations 5 and 6 are directed to Ontario's Ministry of Health and Long-Term Care and the province's Local Health Integration Networks.

THE IMPACT OF CASE MANAGEMENT

The panel recommends that:
1. All MMT programs and prescribing physicians have connections with and access to case management services. [Ia]

THE MMT TEAM

The panel recommends that:
2. Physicians who prescribe MMT endorse the efficacy and value of case management in their dialogue with clients, and collaborate with case management services. Whenever possible, physicians include case

managers in decisions around the admission, discharge and transfer of MMT clients. [IV]

3. Case managers and the other professionals involved in a client's care establish paths of communication and collaboration among themselves. Program structures facilitate the incorporation of this interdisciplinary co-operative approach into practice. [III]

4. Case managers, prescribing physicians, pharmacists and other health care professionals involved in the MMT plan discuss, clarify and agree upon their respective roles, particularly when case management is provided by an agency outside the clinic or office prescribing MMT. [IV]

5. The employers of case managers and others on the MMT team support the therapeutic alliance between the case manager and the client. [III] In recognition that the therapeutic alliance is put at risk and a conflict of interest is introduced when a case manager acts as attendant for urine drug screening, the Ontario Ministry of Health and Long-Term Care develop standards and establish criteria for adequate staffing levels and standards of care in the provision of urine screening. The province's Local Health Integration Networks provide MMT programs with funding to allow them to meet the Ministry standards in staffing and training to support urine screening so that this function does not fall to the case manager by default. [IV]

6. The province's Local Health Integration Networks provide funding for adequate staffing and training so that the MMT team has the resources and skills to deliver a collaborative and solution-focused approach to challenging behaviours that clients may exhibit. [IV]

Assessment and treatment matching

These recommendations address clinical questions 1, 2, 4, 5 and 6. Recommendations 7 to 11 are directed to MMT team members and other professionals who assess clients for methadone maintenance treatment and do treatment matching. Recommendation 12 is directed to the province's Local Health Integration Networks.

INTENSITY OF CASE MANAGEMENT SERVICES

The panel recommends that:

7. Those assessing clients for their suitability for MMT (including intake staff, nurses, physicians and other clinical professionals) facilitate involvement by the case manager at the assessment and beginning stages of treatment so that the case manager can establish contact with the client, begin the engagement and relationship building process, provide information about the kinds of case management services available and discuss with the client what services he or she may need. [III]

8. The client's expectations, perceptions and concerns regarding MMT be discussed and addressed as part of treatment matching, both at the initial assessment and as part of ongoing care. [III]

9. The assessment for MMT incorporate a review of clients' biopsychosocial issues and concerns. [III]

10. Those deciding on the case management services to be provided to clients use a stepped-care approach. Matching treatment needs to service is an essential component of initial assessment and ongoing care in MMT. [III]

11. For clients who are stable and do not require immediate or intensive case management, prescribing physicians consider office-based MMT with formal, established and clear links to case management in place so that it can be accessed if needed. [III]

12. Unstable and high-need clients do better when their methadone treatment, case management and primary medical care, as well as any other related services they may be using, are all located in the same place or as close together as possible. The province's Local Health Integration Networks ensure that this model of care is available for this client group. [IIb]

Core knowledge, competencies and training

These recommendations address clinical questions 1 to 6 and 8. Recommendations 13 to 37 are directed to case managers and the agencies that employ them. Recommendation 13 is also directed to the Ministry of Health and Long-Term Care. Recommendation 25 is also directed to other members of the MMT team. Recommendation 38 is directed to addiction research bodies.

ADDICTION TREATMENT AND MMT

EDUCATION
The panel recommends that:

13. Case managers receive standardized and accredited training in the role and functions of case management, and the Ministry of Health and Long-Term Care develop standards of practice in case management and ensure that educational institutions in Ontario provide accredited training. [IV]

14. Case managers receive standardized and accredited training in, and demonstrate understanding of, the basic principles of opioid dependence, counselling, addiction treatment and MMT, including methadone pharmacology and prescribing protocols. [IV] With the benefit of this training, case managers have the ability to explain to clients how methadone treatment works and provide them with basic information about the College of Physicians and Surgeons of Ontario's prescribing guidelines and the Ontario College of Pharmacists' dispensing guidelines. [III]

COUNSELLING SKILLS AND APPROACHES
The panel recommends that:

15. Case managers receive training and develop skills in motivational interviewing, structured relapse prevention counselling and cognitive-behavioural therapy. [III]

URINE DRUG SCREENING
The panel recommends that:
16. Case managers understand the basic science behind, and the limitations of, urine drug screening and have the ability to clearly explain, to clients and to providers of other social and community services, the issues surrounding the use of urine drug screening and the usefulness of the results in terms of measuring overall client progress. [IV]

POLYSUBSTANCE USE
The panel recommends that:
17. Case managers know the risks of polysubstance use and the health teaching issues surrounding polysubstance use, and apply this knowledge to their assessment of, engagement with and referral of clients with poly-subtance use. [III]

HARM REDUCTION

PROTECTION AND EDUCATION
The panel recommends that:
18. Case managers have knowledge of harm reduction practices, including safer injection, safer sex and overdose protection, and educate their clients about these practices and issues. [III]

19. Case managers ensure that clients have easy and ready access to health education and harm reduction materials and supplies, such as informational literature, condoms and injection and inhalation supplies. [IV]

20. Case managers receive specialized training about the transmission and progression of infection and the psychosocial issues surrounding HIV and hepatitis C. [III]

21. Case managers know about, and liaise with, community resources that can provide services and supports to clients infected with HIV or hepatitis C, and to partners and families. [IV]

22. Case managers assist with, and advocate for, the co-ordination and provision of medical care for clients with HIV or hepatitis C infection. [IV]

23. Because it has been shown that clients who receive outreach and counselling are more likely to re-engage in addiction treatment programs than those who do not receive it [Ib], programs and case managers ensure that clients who drop out of MMT during the early stages of treatment have opportunities to receive ongoing supportive outreach and to resume treatment. [III]

CONFIDENTIALITY AND INFORMATION SHARING

The panel recommends that:
24. Case managers have a demonstrated understanding of the laws and policies that govern the disclosure of information about a client, and operate in accordance with these laws and policies. [IV]

25. Case managers play a role in educating clients about the issues surrounding consent and information sharing. Working with other members of the MMT care team, they ensure that clients understand what information must, by law, be reported to external agencies; how sharing information among members of the MMT care team is beneficial; what their rights are regarding consent for information sharing; and what the implications are of sharing information with external services and third parties (such as employers). Case managers discuss these issues with the client when treatment begins. [IV]

CONCURRENT DISORDERS

The panel recommends that:
26. Case managers demonstrate knowledge of the complex connections between mental health and substance use. [III]

27. Case managers understand the assessment components for concurrent disorders and be able to refer clients to mental health service agencies and/or agencies that treat concurrent disorders. They use collaborative treatment planning strategies to ensure that MMT clients with concurrent disorders receive cohesive and co-ordinated treatment. [IV]

28. Case managers have a demonstrated knowledge of assessment and intervention for suicidality, de-escalation and crisis response. [IV]

TRAUMA

The panel recommends that:

29. Case managers receive basic training in issues of trauma and post-traumatic stress disorder. They have basic skills in handling disclosure, emotional disregulation, escalation and crisis response. [IV]

30. Case managers be aware of the limitations of their own expertise and training and not address trauma issues in an in-depth way unless they have been properly trained to do so and have adequate agency and supervisory support. [IV]

WOMEN, PREGNANCY AND PARENTING

BARRIERS TO WOMEN

The panel recommends that:

31. Case managers receive training and demonstrate awareness of the particular barriers to addiction treatment faced by women, including pregnant and parenting women. [III]

ISSUES FOR PARENTING CLIENTS

The panel recommends that:

32. Case managers act as information and referral agents for pregnant and parenting clients, and link these clients with services and resources that can help them access treatment, pre- and postnatal care and parenting support. [IV]

33. Case managers know and understand the legal and ethical issues involved in the requirement to inform child protection agencies of unstable or unsafe situations for parenting by MMT clients. [IV]

34. Case managers educate other agencies and the health care systems providing care to clients throughout pregnancy, during birth and post-natally about MMT. Case managers advocate on the clients' behalf so that the care they receive is based on informed decisions. [IV]

35. Case managers be aware of the special need for, and apply, an empathic, understanding and non-judgmental approach to interventions with pregnant or parenting clients, to maintain client engagement with treatment. [III]

VIOLENCE

The panel recommends that:

36. Case managers receive training in working with clients who have experienced or are at risk of violence and trauma, specifically training in assessment, safety plans, and available community and legal resources. [III]

EQUITY AND DIVERSITY

The panel recommends that:

37. Agencies and individuals providing case management demonstrate inclusion and awareness of equity and diversity. [IV]

38. Research bodies undertake further study to identify equity and diversity issues and their impact upon best practice of case management in MMT as it applies to Ontario communities and treatment models. [IV]

Program structures

These recommendations address all nine clinical questions. Recommendation 39 is directed to the province's Local Health Integration Networks. Recommendation 43 is directed to the Ontario Ministry of Health and Long-Term Care. Recommendations 40 to 42 and 44 are directed to programs and agencies.

The panel recommends that:

39. The Local Health Integration Networks provide funding to agencies and service providers so that they can implement and incorporate case management best practices into program structures and direct client care. [IV]

SUPPORTING THERAPEUTIC RELATIONSHIPS AND CLIENT ENGAGEMENT

The panel recommends that:

40. Programs are structured and funded so that the workload of case managers allows frequent brief contacts with MMT clients, particularly in the early stages of treatment, to allow relationship building. [III]

41. Programs provide case managers with ongoing supervision and opportunities for reflective practice so that they can continue to develop their therapeutic relationship skills. [IV]

PROGRAM ORIENTATION

The panel recommends that:

42. Methadone providers and programs be educated and aware of the benefits of harm reduction approaches and non-punitive contingency management. [IIb]

43. The Ontario Ministry of Health and Long-Term Care support and require the collection of data, similar to that collected in DATIS, on the different MMT service delivery models and program orientations provided by OHIP-funded providers, and evaluate their outcome measures, including retention and client satisfaction with services. [IV]

LOCATION AND ACCESS TO SERVICES

The panel recommends that:

44. Programs incorporate evening and weekend hours, as well as crisis response services, into their delivery of MMT case management services by partnering with other agencies and resources that provide this service. [IV]

Other health and social services

These recommendations address clinical questions 1 and 4 to 9. Recommendations 45 and 46 are directed to case managers, their employers and other members of the MMT team. Recommendation 47 is directed to health and social service programs. Recommendations 48 and 51 are directed to the Ontario Ministry of Health and Long-Term Care, and Recommendation 51 is also directed to the province's Local Health Integration Networks. Recommendations 48 and 49 are also directed to other funding bodies. Recommendation 50 is directed to hospitals and correctional institutions.

ACCESS TO SERVICES

The panel recommends that:

45. Case managers, with the support of other treatment team members, advocate for improved access to urgent health-care and primary social services (such as shelter and financial support programs) for MMT clients. [III]

46. Case managers, with the support of the MMT team, act as referral agents to these service agencies and co-ordinate the delivery of their services. [III]

FOSTERING INCLUSIVITY

The panel recommends that:

47. All health and social service programs in Ontario be accessible to and inclusive of MMT clients. [IV]

48. The Ontario Ministry of Health and Long-Term Care and other funding bodies provide funding for awareness education and service mechanisms to social service programs, to assist them with making their services more inclusive of MMT clients. [IV]

49. Government programs and other bodies funding employment and vocational training programs identify and reduce barriers to their services for MMT clients. [III]

INSTITUTIONAL BARRIERS

The panel recommends that:

50. Hospitals and correctional institutions function with an awareness of the direct impact that the continuity and consistency of methadone dosing has on clients within their systems. They ensure that their admission and discharge planning procedures allow clients timely access to their daily methadone dose. These institutions implement and standardize collaboration and communication processes with case managers so that clients receive seamless care and consistent dosing. [IV]

51. The Ontario Ministry of Health and Long-Term Care and the province's Local Health Integration Networks fund research to evaluate, or require funded agencies to evaluate, the systemic barriers to accessing health and social services for MMT clients in Ontario, and use this data to improve these services. [IV]

Technology and telemedicine

This recommendation addresses clinical questions 1, 4 and 7 to 9. Recommendation 52 is directed to the Ontario Ministry of Health and Long-Term Care.

The panel recommends that:

52. The Ontario Ministry of Health and Long-Term Care ensure that evaluation and outcome measures associated with the use of technology, particularly telemedicine, including levels of client satisfaction, be available and used by these service programs delivering MMT case management services. [IV]

The role of case management in MMT

Case management remains a loosely defined service that, in practice, lends itself to many adaptations to achieve a variety of objectives, as discussed in Ridgely and Willenbring (1992). Broadly speaking, the case manager functions as the co-ordinating hub at the centre of a circle of care for clients in MMT. He or she co-ordinates treatment, provides links to information and a wide range of resources, facilitates the client's access both to any additional health care needed and to other kinds of services, and acts as an advocate for the client.

CLIENT CONSULTATION FINDINGS

WHAT SERVICES DO CLIENTS WANT FROM CASE MANAGERS?

From a list of 30 functions or services typically provided by case managers, these are the top 10 that clients either received or wanted to receive:
1. Help with changing drug and alcohol use
2. Support and someone to talk to; general counselling
3. Help with a health issue such as hepatitis C, HIV, birth control, access to health care
4. Help with lifestyle changes such as smoking, nutrition, exercise, leisure time
5. Help with a mental health issue such as depression or anxiety
6. Help with a crisis
7. Help with referrals to community resources, filling out forms and applications, providing letters
8. Help with a family or relationship problem
9. Help with understanding MMT and adjusting to the program
10. Help with a legal issue such as court or probation

A case manager's function encompasses a range of activities. The more flexible and wide-ranging these activities are, the greater the likelihood that clients will remain engaged in treatment (Potik et al., 2007).

Working with MMT clients can be complex. Not only are clients making changes in how they use substances but they often present with an array of other issues. Some are the direct result of their use of substances (for example, financial, legal and health problems); some may have existed before the onset of substance use (such as trauma, mental health problems or relationship difficulties) and some are associated with other social factors affecting the client's life (such as poverty, illiteracy, racism, gender oppression, stigma and so on).

Further complications result from the pharmacology of methadone and the issues associated with prescribing and ingesting it, as well as from the various constraints, regulations and compliance issues unique to MMT. Some programs make additional demands on clients in terms of access to services, and in some cases misinformation and bias about methadone treatment is widespread even within the systems of care with which the client—and therefore the case manager—must contend.

Additionally, case managers often face high workloads and significant time constraints, which can limit clients' access to their services.

SIZE OF CASELOAD

There are no studies in Canada that address the question of optimal caseload for MMT case managers, and no single answer: much depends on the type of service offered, the range of other community supports available and the needs of the client.

Anecdotal reports suggest the caseloads of managers in many MMT programs in Ontario range from 40 to 300 clients. Assertive community treatment teams (ACT teams) that provide intense case management to high-need clients within the mental health system report caseloads of 10 to 15 clients per case manager. Community mental health agencies that provide moderate

support to clients with mental health problems living in the
community report caseloads of 15 to 25 clients per case manager.

The Addiction Research Foundation (now part of the Centre for
Addiction and Mental Health) opened one of the first methadone
programs in Ontario in 1971. Its case managers averaged 30 to 40
cases each up until 1995. From 1995 to the present, this program
averaged 50 to 60 cases per case manager. (This is a high-service
clinic with multiple onsite resources and a mandate of accepting
only complex and high-need clients.)

Case management involves co-ordinating a continuity of care and
support to ensure that the multiple needs of the client are addressed.
It is longitudinal, moving in step with and adapting to the client as he or
she makes progress over time, even when the specifics of service sites
and caregivers change. Case management focuses on the removal of
barriers and obstacles. Good case management must be individualized,
comprehensive, flexible and personal, built on a positive therapeutic
relationship between the client and the care provider.

The case manager may be expected either to link to services or to actually
provide the bulk of services, depending on the resources and availability
of services within the centre and community in which he or she is practising.
The case manager is the member of the MMT team who is often in the best
position, because of his or her connections with other community services,
to look at the overall picture of the client's individual circumstances and
needs and to then develop a plan to manage the care and support to address
those needs. Case management is especially useful in the treatment of
clients with severe and complex problems that involve multiple service
agencies (Kirk & Therrien, 1975; Bachrach, 1978, 1981, 1989 [all cited in
Ridgely & Willenbring, 1992]).

There is widespread agreement that best practice calls for a case manager
to perform the functions of assessment, planning, referring (or otherwise
linking), monitoring, general counselling, advocacy and outreach (Phillips
et al., 1988; Ontario MOHLTC, 1985; Austin, 1983; Schwartz et al., 1982;
Lamb, 1980; Marshman, 1978 [all cited in Ridgely & Willenbring, 1992]).

Table 5 shows the components of case management in MMT within agencies funded by the Ontario Ministry of Health and Long-Term Care. Case managers working for agencies funded by the Ministry use these categories to describe the work they do when reporting on their program activities.

TABLE 5

Components of case management in MMT*

DIRECT CONTACT

Practical help	• assisting with daily activities • linking and co-ordinating necessary services
Crisis/drop-in	• responding immediately in urgent situations • providing assistance, advice and support
Monitoring/support	• checking in • offering general support
Treatment planning	• negotiating client's treatment plan with client and other providers

INDIRECT CONTACT

Case conferences	• meeting or consulting regarding client with co-providers or referents
Service co-ordination/ consultation	• referring to external agencies • co-ordinating services
Advocacy	• advocating with other agencies or organizations on behalf of client

*As recognized in the Drug and Alcohol Treatment Information System (www.datis.ca) database used by agencies funded by the Ontario Ministry of Health and Long-Term Care.

THE IMPACT OF CASE MANAGEMENT

The panel recommends that:
1. All MMT programs and prescribing physicians have connections with and access to case management services. [1a]

The positive effect on treatment outcomes of including case management and counselling services in the delivery of MMT has been well documented in the literature. Specifically, the provision of these services enhances treatment retention, decreases clients' use of illegal opioids and other substances and improves clients' overall functioning in terms of criminality, homelessness, mental health and vocational and educational involvement (Health Canada, 2002a).

MMT programs that include some form of case management and counselling have been shown to have superior results to those that provide methadone as a "stand-alone" intervention, as measured by outcomes that include:
- program retention
- reduction in high-risk behaviour (such as injection and illegal activity)
- greater levels of social stability (in terms of employment and housing)
- reduced incidents of mental health crisis incidents (such as suicide attempts or hospitalization)
- reductions in opioid and other substance use.

(Ball & Ross, 1991; Health Canada, 2002a; Bell, 1998; Leshner, 1999; Gossop, Stewart et al., 2006; Warj et al., 1992; Laken & Ager, 1996; Kay & Peters, 1992).

As established in 1983 by McLellan et al.'s study on the effect of psychosocial services on the treatment outcomes of clients with a broad range of substance use issues, outcomes are improved across all groups when clients have access to health and other social services and there is some follow-up on their service use. Other studies and reports have similarly documented improved outcomes and treatment retention among substance users who have access to the supports and resources that are part of case management services (Health Canada, 1999; APA, 2006; Mayet et al., 2008).

CLIENT CONSULTATION FINDINGS

WHO PROVIDES CASE MANAGEMENT AND COUNSELLING?

- Of the surveyed clients who received case management, the vast majority (98%) indicated that they received it from a designated worker or case manager (either within their methadone program, at another agency or both).
- More than 80% of the clients received case management and counselling services that were directly connected to their methadone programs.
- Approximately 35% of the clients received additional counselling and case management services at another agency.
- 27% received counselling and case management from their doctors (either alone or in addition to other support).
- 18% received counselling and case management from a nurse (either connected to their methadone treatment or at another agency, and either alone or in connection with other services).
- 12% received counselling from a psychiatrist (either alone or in addition to services from another agency).

PRACTICE POINT

INITIAL CLIENT ENCOUNTERS

- Give your clients a clear description of your role and function as a case manager. Provide clear and practical examples of tasks you are able to help with, such as completing forms and applications, finding housing and connecting to other social service systems.
- Explore with clients how staying in treatment can sometimes feel challenging and overwhelming, and discuss the kind of counselling or practical support they might find helpful. Explore their perceptions and beliefs about MMT as a holistic treatment.
- Talk about how regular, brief contact with you to discuss how things are going for them might be helpful.
- Acknowledge that clients need to work at their own pace.

CLIENT CONSULTATION FINDINGS

BENEFITS OF CASE MANAGEMENT

Clients reported the three most helpful things about case management services:
1. "Feeling like someone understands and supports me."
2. "Helping me make changes in my life."
3. "Help with a crisis."

CLIENT CONSULTATION FINDINGS

CHALLENGES IN CASE MANAGEMENT

Clients reported the top three challenges in working with their case managers:
1. It was difficult to form a trusting relationship.
2. The case manager was not available in emergencies.
3. The case manager was not as available as the client would have liked.

CLIENTS TALK ABOUT
COUNSELLING AND CASE MANAGEMENT

"This clinic used to have counselling but they don't anymore. I'm trying to arrange it through another agency."

"I wanted to see a counsellor in my community but he only comes in from another town a few days per week. I had other appointments and other things to do, so I have not been able to connect yet. He is really booked up. It's hard for me to travel out of town to see a counsellor."

"Counselling is limited, you have to ask for it, nothing is formal or arranged."

"When I started methadone 15 years ago there wasn't much case management—but now it's part of my program."

"I'm on a list to see a counsellor in my community. It's been over five months so far."

"I had another therapist—private psychotherapy—but could no longer afford it; it wasn't covered."

"I got counselling in jail. When I got out, the MMT program didn't have counselling and I could not get in to see a counsellor in the community because of wait-lists."

"[There should be m]ore one-on-one counselling. I have lots of issues that are sensitive and you can't always do it in a group. Wait-lists for mental health services are really long."

"Having counsellors available is important. Also important [is] to have counselling available not directly in your community where everyone knows everyone. This would make it easier."

THE MMT TEAM

Collaborative interprofessional care in health services in general has been demonstrated to:
- improve patient outcomes
- reduce costs
- shorten wait times
- lower rates of staff burnout and turnover.

In Ontario, the collaborative model of care is the guiding best practice for hospitals and other health care service delivery systems (Ontario MOHLTC, 2008).

Collaborative practice in MMT is recommended by the licensing body for prescribers in Ontario (CPSO, 2005), but no regulated service delivery model for MMT case management currently exists in the province.

Numerous best practice guides also emphasize the importance of communication and collaboration among physicians, pharmacists, case managers and other MMT program service staff (Health Canada, 2002a; SSAM, 2007; NIDA, 1999b; Farrell et al., 1996). Good communication and effective collaboration is seen as essential to providing seamless and comprehensive client care (Ontario MOHLTC, 2008).

IMPROVING COMMUNICATION AMONG TEAM MEMBERS

Pharmacists, doctors, nurses and case managers can improve how they communicate in a number of ways, including:

- holding regular team meetings or rounds and quick "red flag" communication about urgent client care issues (telephone, online, e-mail and remote conferencing mechanisms are ideal provided they are secure and do not compromise client confidentiality)
- having case managers (with the clients' permission) sit in occasionally on doctor/client appointments, and/or have doctors or nurses occasionally sit in on case manager/client appointments
- establishing a central place (such as a care plan folder in each client's file) where documentation and communication about treatment issues and plans can be accessed by all of the care providers.

In Ontario, how prescribers and pharmacists communicate and collaborate with case managers on treatment planning varies. Some function as true treatment teams, with regular communication and agreements about client care; others are loosely associated "silos" of service in different locations, run by a mix of social service agencies, private enterprise and individualized practice models, with vaguely defined or no communication, treatment-planning and integration strategies.

The panel recommends that:

2. Physicians who prescribe MMT endorse the efficacy and value of case management in their dialogue with clients, and collaborate with case management services. Whenever possible, physicians include case managers in decisions around the admission, discharge and transfer of MMT clients. [IV]

3. Case managers and the other professionals involved in a client's care establish paths of communication and collaboration among themselves. Program structures facilitate the incorporation of this interdisciplinary co-operative approach into practice. [III]

SAM

SCENARIO: Sam is a 32-year-old client with a lengthy history of prescription opioid dependence; he has been on methadone for two years. His urine drug screening results frequently show positive for opioids, and he has been able to obtain only one take-home dose a week, and only for brief periods of time. Recently, several other clients have complained that Sam has been dealing drugs outside the clinic. Sam's methadone doctor is concerned about this turn of events and wonders if keeping Sam on the program will negatively affect other clients who come to the clinic.

REFLECTION: Sam's doctor understands that involving case management services in decisions about client continuance in the program, as well as in any dialogue with clients, is helpful. He discusses his concerns with Sam's case manager and they decide to meet with Sam together to review the concerns and work out a plan.

RESPONSE: The case manager understands that a team approach to making decisions about client discharge or transfer is a best practice. She agrees to work with Sam and the doctor to draw up a behavioural contract. The case manager also invites Sam to share his perspectives on how treatment is going for him, what

---

Continued on page 55

Continued from page 54

other supports he might find helpful and whether he requires practical assistance with finances, obtaining housing or work training. During the dialogue, Sam admits that he is facing increasing financial pressures as he has not been able to work at his casual job and owes "lots of money." He also admits that he is feeling stressed and anxious and that he uses illegal opioids to cope with these feelings.

The case manager and doctor explore possible solutions with Sam, including increased case management contact to help him address some of these issues. Both the case manager and the doctor stress how important it is for Sam to adhere to a behavioural contract in which he agrees not to sell drugs on clinic property, but they also express the concern they have for him, the supports they are prepared to offer and their wish to help him succeed on the program. Sam is encouraged to keep working closely with his case manager and they all agree to check in weekly about how Sam is progressing.

WHO IS ON AN MMT TEAM?

The MMT team in the circle of care around a client may include:
- the prescribing physician
- a program nurse involved in primary client care
- associated program staff (intake workers, urine screening attendants)
- the dispensing pharmacist
- the case manager.

PRACTICE POINT

MMT IS A HOLISTIC TREATMENT

MMT works best when all members of the treatment team recognize its holistic nature and strive to keep each other informed and involved. Communication with clients should also reflect this principle of collaboration. In particular, physicians making decisions about client discharge, transfer or other significant issues that may affect a client's continuance in the program are encouraged to discuss and implement these decisions in a manner that involves all members of the treatment team.

CLIENTS TALK ABOUT
THEIR EXPERIENCES WITH PHARMACIES

"Be more understanding about people on methadone. [At the pharmacy t]hey put other customers first. Sometimes I've waited all day to have my methadone prescription filled. By 3:00 p.m. I'm feeling rough . . . when I dropped it off at 9:00 a.m."

"I went in the store one day with my sunglasses and my hood up and [the pharmacist] told me to take them off because I looked like I was going to rob the place. It's how I normally dress. He ended up apologizing to me a few days later."

"I would be at the front of the line at the pharmacy and then often people would come after me and get served first. I told them I didn't like it and we worked it out. It's been better for the last month. I can't sit or stand for long, as I use a cane and waiting was very difficult for me."

"The pharmacy staff was very helpful when I started out. They were very encouraging. I didn't feel well at first but they helped me hang in there."

"I can call the pharmacist on the phone if I have questions. They have been really good that way."

"They are really friendly; they phone the doctor for me about my other medication."

"The area where the pharmacy is, is a rough area. I've been stopped by the police several times and been accused of working there. If I had a choice, I wouldn't be in this area."

"Being in line for pharmacy isn't good. People fight physically, deal drugs, talk about drugs. You see bad things when you are trying to get sober. It's easy for me to get drugs here. I was a witness to a woman beating her daughter. I had to give a report to the police. Now she drinks her methadone here and it's very uncomfortable. The scene here can be very intense. It's not a safe place, especially for children. Mothers bring children here all the time."

"I couldn't make the $6 payment [for my dose] and they wouldn't accept partial payment. They would not dose me. I had to get advocacy to get my dose. I only had $3 that day but they would not accept that, even though I was getting paid the next day and was going to bring it in."

PRACTICE POINT

SUPPORTING THE CLIENT/PHARMACY RELATIONSHIP

- Be aware that clients' experiences at the pharmacy can be challenging and may evoke emotionally charged responses. Check in with them about their experiences; check in with the pharmacists, too.
- Be an active participant in resolving any problems, and encourage clients to develop their own problem-solving and communication skills.
- Help clients prepare to deal with potentially difficult or triggering situations.

CLIENT CONSULTATION FINDINGS

PHARMACY EXPERIENCES

- Of the clients surveyed, 80% reported that the lack of privacy (taking their medication or talking to the pharmacist in a public rather than a private space) was the most challenging issue for them at pharmacies.
- Nearly half of the clients surveyed (45%) cited restrictive hours at pharmacies as a concern.
- Nine out of 10 clients reported that a caring attitude and courteous, non-judgmental staff were the most positive aspects of dealing with the pharmacies where they drank their methadone.
- About 60% reported that learning from the pharmacist—about methadone, its potential risks and side effects, safety and what to expect from treatment—was a positive aspect of their pharmacy experience.

The panel recommends that:

4. Case managers, prescribing physicians, pharmacists and other health care professionals involved in the MMT plan discuss, clarify and agree upon their respective roles, particularly when case management is provided by an agency outside the clinic or office prescribing MMT. [IV]

Clear boundaries around the role of the case manager are sometimes difficult to establish. Case managers may be called upon to perform various functions depending on the resources of the clinic and local community. Often, case managers report that they experience conflict between the roles that have been shown to be best practice for the job and the roles that fall to them by default, perhaps because of lack of adequate staffing or other resources in the environment in which they work. Many programs acknowledge that the provision of case management and counselling enhances treatment outcome, but are not able to provide these services due to fiscal and resource constraints (Lilly et al., 1999; Farrell et al., 1996).

Further, case managers may be required by their employers or by conditions in their work environment to take on duties that are not consistent with case management best practices, for example, "policing" clients' compliance with program expectations and guidelines (such as confronting clients about missed pharmacy payments, being asked to patrol the areas in and outside of the clinic for people who may be using drugs); at the same time, they may not always be able to provide core case management and counselling services because of time constraints created by either these extraneous duties or by excessive caseloads (Lilly et al., 1999; Farrell et al., 1996). Stewart et al. (2004) found that the high demand for case management, coupled with the shortage of resources to meet this demand, may affect treatment retention and the discharge policies of individual programs; they recommend further exploration of this issue.

Fischer et al. (2002) report that in a survey of Ontario MMT physicians, 64 per cent of respondents felt that there were inadequate counselling and social service resources in the methadone treatment system. Of the respondents, 42 per cent indicated that the provision of counselling services for methadone clients was the most urgent need in the methadone treatment system, and 23 per cent said that general social service resources were the most urgent need.

Clients vary greatly in their need for case management services. Their needs can fluctuate over time and are sometimes dependent on moving in and out of crisis situations, relapsing or encountering other urgent issues. A small caseload of high-need, unstable clients may be more demanding of the case manager's time than a large caseload of relatively stable clients. A good measure of adequate caseload-to-case-manager ratio is whether the clients and the case manager have time to connect with each other and work together on the client's treatment plan or emergent issues, and whether the case manager has adequate time to complete tasks such as paperwork, documentation, referral and linking activities (the "management" part of case management) and to communicate effectively with the rest of the MMT care team regarding the client's care. Absolute numbers are misleading.

The panel recommends that:

5. The employers of case managers and others on the MMT team support the therapeutic alliance between the case manager and the client. [III] In recognition that the therapeutic alliance is put at risk and a conflict of interest is introduced when a case manager acts as attendant for urine drug screening, the Ontario Ministry of Health and Long-Term Care develop standards and establish criteria for adequate staffing levels and standards of care in the provision of urine screening. The province's Local Health Integration Networks provide MMT programs with funding to allow them to meet the Ministry standards in staffing and training to support urine screening so that this function does not fall to the case manager by default. [IV]

Urine drug screening typically involves an attendant supervising the client's urinating (to provide the sample), either through direct observation in the bathroom with the client or with the use of video cameras or two-way mirrors.

In some MMT programs in Ontario, case managers are asked to perform this urine screening attendant function due to lack of program resources. While no direct research was found on how this role affects the therapeutic relationship and alliance, on the basis of expert opinion and anecdotal reports from clients about their difficulty in forming a trusting relationship with their case managers, the advisory panel cautions against this use of case managers. In Western culture, voiding is largely considered a private act, and a case manager's observation is perceived as crossing a personal boundary in a way that frequently affects the therapeutic alliance. There is no hard evidence to suggest that such observation by a case manager increases clients' shame or lowers their self-esteem, but in the absence of such research we cannot assume that it does not. The advisory panel views this function as introducing a conflict of interest. There seems to be no other function in case management or counselling where observing an intimate physical act is performed routinely as part of care.

Not all clients have difficult experiences with observed urine screens, nor do all have difficult relationships with those whose specific job it is to observe urine drug screening (urine screening attendants). Many clients are comfortable with urine screening attendants and develop good relationships with them, but these relationships are different from the type of relationship in which counselling, case management or therapeutic intervention can take place.

The panel recommends that:

6. The province's Local Health Integration Networks provide funding for adequate staffing and training so that the MMT team has the resources and skills to deliver a collaborative and solution-focused approach to challenging behaviours that clients may exhibit. [IV]

POLICING VS. PROBLEM-SOLVING

SCENARIO: The case manager receives a call from a community pharmacist, who tells her that a small group of MMT clients regularly congregate outside her store, loitering for lengthy periods of time. The pharmacist says that she has clients sign a behavioural agreement when they first start receiving their methadone at her pharmacy; however, this group of clients has ignored her reminders about the agreement and her requests to not loiter. The pharmacist asks the case manager to do something about this situation—otherwise she will no longer provide dispensing services to these clients.

REFLECTION: The case manager understands that MMT works best when there is communication and collaboration among all members of the team, and that rigid "policing" of the "rules" of MMT can have a negative impact on therapeutic relationships. She knows the team needs to understand and agree upon clear expectations of their respective roles.

RESPONSE: The case manager offers to work with the pharmacist, starting by talking with clients about alternatives to congregating around the entrance to the store. She explores with the pharmacist and the clients why the loitering is problematic, and encourages

Continued on page 62

Continued from page 61

the clients to identify the barriers to their compliance—that is, how she and the pharmacist can help them succeed in complying with the behavioural contract. The case manager, in discussion with the pharmacist, explores factors that contribute to the loitering, such as the clients needing to wait for rides back home, and encourages a problem-solving approach from both the clients and the pharmacist. She encourages the pharmacist to communicate her concerns to the prescribing physician as well, and then suggests regular three-way communication to monitor the situation.

Assessment and treatment matching

Not all clients require case management, and the needs of those who do may change in intensity as their treatment progresses. Providing clients with easy and timely access to case management services, particularly for the early stages (during assessment and treatment induction), improves treatment outcome and increases retention. Exploring clients' expectations of MMT and their prior experiences with case management and counselling may alleviate some of the ambivalence they often have about MMT and can also improve their level of engagement and the likelihood of their staying in treatment. These aims can be achieved by structuring programs so that they support the case manager's connection to the client during the initial assessment and the beginning of treatment.

INTENSITY OF CASE MANAGEMENT SERVICES

MMT programs vary in the duration and range of case management and/or counselling services they offer. Programs that offer services beyond the prescription of methadone generally produce more positive results, although there appears to be a threshold beyond which more frequent or higher levels of services are not more effective. Not all clients require the same level of counselling and case management involvement to achieve positive outcomes (Kidorf et al., 2004; Gossop, Stewart et al., 2006; Seivewright et al., 2000, pp. 164–166; Warj et al., 1992; Dennis et al., 1992; Health Canada, 2002a; Woody et al., 1995; McLellan et al., 2005).

The panel recommends that:

7. Those assessing clients for their suitability for MMT (including intake staff, nurses, physicians and other clinical professionals) facilitate involvement by the case manager at the assessment and beginning stages of treatment so that the case manager can establish contact with the client, begin the engagement and relationship building process, provide information about the kinds of case management services available and discuss with the client what services he or she may need. [III]

Early intervention by case managers and early engagement by clients in the case management or counselling process have been shown to increase retention rates. Treatment retention, in turn, has been shown to have a direct correlation with reduced mortality and decreases in illegal substance use (Dzialdowski et al., 1998; Gossop et al., 2003; Woody et al., 2007).

The panel recommends that:

8. The client's expectations, perceptions and concerns regarding MMT be discussed and addressed as part of treatment matching, both at the initial assessment and as part of ongoing care. [III]

9. The assessment for MMT incorporate a review of clients' biopsychosocial issues and concerns. [III]

Client attitudes, expectations and perceptions of MMT prior to beginning treatment are important indicators of future success. Negative attitudes toward and perceptions of MMT are associated with higher drop-out rates. Early intervention and exploration of these attitudes can result in an attitudinal shift for clients, encouraging treatment retention and program engagement (Gossop et al., 2003; Kayman et al., 2006; Futterman et al., 2005; Meichenbaum & Turk, 1987; Giyaur et al., 2005; Madden et al., 2008; Booth et al., 2004).

JOHN

SCENARIO: John is a 43-year-old client with a 15-year history of dependence on prescription opioids. He began MMT three weeks ago and his dose is still being titrated to eliminate withdrawal symptoms. John met his case manager briefly when he met with his doctor after his first dose. He expressed hope and enthusiasm about being on MMT and said that since he had a job and supportive family, he didn't need to see the case manager again "because everything is going to be great."

The case manager meets with John two weeks later to see how things are going. Now John tells her, "This isn't working for me. I still feel really sick from withdrawal and I want to use. I came here to feel better, to stop using and get my life on track. But all I do is travel down here to meet the doctor, then stand in line at the pharmacy and to leave urine screens, and I feel sick and shaky all day. Plus a couple of times on my way here people have asked me if I want to buy drugs or extra methadone. I'm in trouble at work because I keep missing time and leaving early because I don't feel well. I really don't know if I want to be tied to this clinic and this program. I thought once I started treatment things would be different, but I've still got all the stress."

REFLECTION: The case manager recognizes that John had certain expectations about MMT and that the reality of his experience is different. John has some concerns about the environment where his treatment program is located and doubts his ability to manage the program's demands. The case manager also realizes that John is at risk for dropping out if he cannot resolve his negative feelings about his experience thus far.

RESPONSE: The case manager validates John's frustrations and concerns. She explains to John how getting started on MMT can be very demanding, but also points out how things may improve if he can manage to cope during this difficult time. She explores strategies with John about how he can negotiate time off with his employer and cope with the stress of daily attendance at the clinic. She also talks with him about how he can respond when people ask him if he wants to buy illegal drugs. She asks John what could make his visits at the clinic more positive and suggests they check in with each other a few times a week to see how he is adjusting to the program.

CLIENTS TALK ABOUT
STARTING MMT

"I would have liked to know more about methadone before I started. It would have helped me make a better decision. You shouldn't just tell a sick person 'this will make you better.' "

"Sometimes I feel like I'm being penalized for using. I don't think they understand. It's not as easy as saying 'no.' I feel like I'm being held hostage—methadone is hard-core stuff."

"When you stop using, you end up being isolated. It would be helpful to have more help with exercise and general activity programs. I try to do this on my own but it's hard. More help with this would be good."

"Programs should be more flexible and lenient and work with people. Counselling should be more one on one; groups are not always the best place, and some people don't function well in groups."

"Realize that people are individuals and different. Especially when they are starting the program, be reassuring; make them feel like they don't have to be scared or embarrassed. Help them know that their MMT team is on their side and is going to go to bat for them. Let them know that they will get help not just with the addiction but with other issues as well. Remember what the person is feeling, especially when starting."

MMT AND SPECIAL POPULATIONS: YOUTH

The CPSO guidelines (2005) recommend that if circumstances warrant starting a young person (under age 18) on methadone, the treatment must be carried out in consultation with a physician knowledgeable in adolescent addiction medicine.

Case managers are advised to work closely with all of the health care providers involved with a youth client to ensure integrated care.

Case managers should approach the case management of adolescents in MMT as they would for any other clients in terms of:
- access to case management
- empathic and respectful client-centred approaches
- referral and support to community agencies and services.

Recommended skills and knowledge that can enhance case management work with youth include:
- family counselling skills
- an understanding of issues regarding informed consent for the treatment of minors
- an awareness of the stigma experienced by adolescent substance users and their families
- an understanding of biopsychosocial issues affecting adolescent substance users, including mental health and developmental issues unique to this group
- the ability to connect and collaborate with other systems that the client may be involved with, such as school, young offender programs and supportive housing programs for youth
- consideration of the impact that attendance at a methadone clinic setting may have on the client in terms of exposure and association with more seasoned adult users
- a commitment to ongoing learning based on emergent research about adolescent substance use.

PRACTICE POINT

EARLY STAGES OF TREATMENT

- Connect early with clients and discuss any concerns they have about their treatment. Explore the disparity between what they had thought treatment would be like and how it's turning out.
- If clients find treatment challenging initially, acknowledge their difficulties and praise them for sticking with it. Celebrate even small successes (such as daily attendance to pick up the methadone dose, keeping appointments, etc.).
- Provide practical assistance with anything identified by the client as a potential barrier to continuing in the program, such as travel arrangements, food and housing issues, applications for financial support, etc.

The panel recommends that:

10. Those deciding on the case management services to be provided to clients use a stepped-care approach. Matching treatment needs to service is an essential component of initial assessment and ongoing care in MMT. [III]

11. For clients who are stable and do not require immediate or intensive case management, prescribing physicians consider office-based MMT with formal, established and clear links to case management in place so that it can be accessed if needed. [III]

Comprehensive care should be available and accessible to clients to the degree that they need it. This can mean "stepped care"—for example, moving stable MMT clients out of a methadone clinic environment to office-based care, as long as access to case management is still available as needed. Office-based MMT puts stable clients back into the familiar, "normal" environment of the family doctor practice, thereby helping to alleviate some of the stigma that may accompany attendance at an MMT-focused clinic or program centre. Moving to office-based care also removes stable clients from others whose use might act as triggers for them.

Office-based MMT also provides a way to provide methadone treatment to clients in communities where clinics do not exist. Co-operation and communication between pharmacies and prescribing MMT physicians is essential in order for office-based MMT to work well (Newfoundland & Labrador Pharmacy Board, 2007).

In the absence of office or community resources, Drucker et al. (2007) recommend that physicians be willing and able to provide counselling and referral, although this approach is appropriate only for stable clients.

SERVICES AT OFFICE-BASED MMT PRACTICES

Generally, "office-based MMT practice" refers to a general practitioner who prescribes methadone for MMT and who may or may not have in-house supports or formalized community partnerships to provide case management. There is no standard for office-based practice in Ontario regarding what other services are or should be included (besides the prescription of methadone and all that it entails).

CLIENTS TALK ABOUT
CASE MANAGERS AND DOCTORS

"My doctor gives me counselling—sometimes for practical things, my case manager will help out."

"Case management is really important, as well as the right doctor. The doctor follows you body-wise, the counsellor asks questions about how you are doing in other areas. They pick up on things."

The panel recommends that:
12. Unstable and high-need clients do better when their methadone treatment, case management and primary medical care, as well as any other related services they may be using, are all located in the same place or as close together as possible. The province's Local Health Integration Networks ensure that this model of care is available for this client group. [IIb]

For some client populations, making primary medical care services available in proximity to MMT treatment locations and improving access to these services have been shown to increase client use of the services and decrease use of emergency rooms and other high-cost services (Friedmann et al., 2006; Gourevitch et al., 2007).

Locating case management services on the same site as primary medical care also appears to increase high-need unstable clients' use of services, particularly in the areas of financial assistance, advocacy and housing (Friedmann et al., 2000).

CLIENT CONSULTATION FINDINGS

FALLING THROUGH THE CRACKS

Of the clients surveyed, 15% stated that case management services were not able to help them with complex issues.

This finding suggests that for a small group of clients, there are significant barriers to accessing or benefiting from case management services, sometimes resulting in the service needs going unmet. These barriers include wait-lists, resource scarcity and a high level of need.

While the number of MMT clients in this situation—needing more specialized services or unusually high levels of help with accessing those resources—may be small, the barriers facing them are significant. It is possible that the unmet case management and other resource needs of this group of clients results in their being less stable and, ultimately, resulting in proportionally greater social, medical and legal costs.

Tracking the needs of clients with complex issues that fall outside of the mainstream service spectrum is an urgent research and resource issue.

JASON

SCENARIO: Jason is a 35-year-old oral opioid user with schizophrenia. He frequently stops taking his psychiatric medication and cycles in and out of shelters and boarding homes. Jason also has hepatitis C and poorly controlled diabetes. He frequently misses appointments with his various care providers and does not eat properly or manage his finances successfully. He recently was started on methadone in a stand-alone methadone-only clinic, but has not been doing well. He is a frequent visitor to the local emergency room, seeking medication when he has not had his methadone dose for a few days. He has been referred by the hospital staff to case management services at a local community health centre because they have been unable to help Jason make lasting changes and have requested that he no longer come to the emergency room when he has issues with his medication.

REFLECTION: The case manager understands that clients who are highly unstable with multiple needs and chaotic lifestyles have better outcomes when all of their primary medical and mental health services and their methadone treatment are in one location.

RESPONSE: The case manager arranges to have Jason's methadone care as well as his mental health care and medical care transferred to a community health clinic. Here, Jason can come for his methadone, see a nurse for his diabetes and hepatitis C follow-up, and get his methadone and other medication prescribed by a primary care physician. The case manager also arranges for Jason to fill all of his prescriptions at the pharmacy close to the clinic, and helps him enrol in some of the clinic's health and social programs, such as community cooking, foot care and peer support groups.

CLIENTS TALK ABOUT
CONNECTING TO OTHER RESOURCES AND SUPPORTS

"I had depression but they told me I have to go and find a psychiatrist by myself. I didn't know how to do that. I spent a long time without medications. They should hook you up with that. I saw a nurse practitioner at agency Q but that was only for a few weeks of meds. It's actually on your own shoulders. They should offer more services. If you are giving someone methadone, you should have more support. The people here are very friendly but it's not enough. I thought there would be more support."

"It really helps if they [the case manager] come to appointments with me, especially medical ones. I won't go unless they come with me. I know for my blood work, it's important that the person taking my blood listens to me. That is why having the worker here is helpful."

"Getting started on the hep C treatment was very difficult. I didn't feel I had the support I needed."

"I have chronic pain issues, possibly Crohn's disease, and I find it difficult to cope physically or emotionally. More counselling and medical help would be good, to help me deal with stress."

PRACTICE POINT

ASSESSING OVERALL STABILITY

Besides doing a thorough assessment and treatment plan for a client's opioid dependency, the case manager needs to establish how well the client is functioning in other areas of his or her life. A client's instability or difficulty in one or more of the following areas may indicate that he or she may benefit from a more intensive and direct connection to case management services:
- high-risk injection behaviour
- polysubstance use
- co-occurring mental illness
- chronic physical health problems
- social isolation
- unstable housing
- inadequate resources for basic self-care, such as food
- relationship violence
- involvement in the criminal justice system
- involvement with child protection agencies
- pregnancy
- chaotic lifestyle (frequently missed appointments or doses)

Core knowledge, competencies and training

ADDICTION TREATMENT AND MMT

EDUCATION

The panel recommends that:

13. Case managers receive standardized and accredited training in the role and functions of case management, and the Ministry of Health and Long-Term Care develop standards of practice in case management and ensure that educational institutions in Ontario provide accredited training. [IV]

Brown and Dongier (2005) found that in Canada substance use counsellors and case managers are not always accredited, and have varying degrees of education; they recommend improved training and accreditation of counsellors and case managers. There is a similar lack of accreditation, standards and training in other countries (Farrell et al., 1996).

A WIDE RANGE OF BACKGROUNDS

No accurate inventory or research on the education and professional affiliation of case managers in Ontario MMT programs has been documented. Anecdotal reports suggest that they come from a variety of backgrounds and educational paths, including social work, social service work, human services work, mental health work, nursing, psychology, community work, lived recovery and peer education work.

The panel recommends that:

14. Case managers receive standardized and accredited training in, and demonstrate understanding of, the basic principles of opioid dependence, counselling, addiction treatment and M M T, including methadone pharmacology and prescribing protocols. [IV] With the benefit of this training, case managers have the ability to explain to clients how methadone treatment works and provide them with basic information about the College of Physicians and Surgeons of Ontario's prescribing guidelines and the Ontario College of Pharmacists' dispensing guidelines. [III]

Opioid use and its treatment with methadone involves a well-defined, regulated medical protocol. It is important that case managers understand how methadone works pharmacologically and be familiar with the guidelines for and restrictions on prescribing it (Hagman, 1994 [as cited in Martin et al., 2003], ssam, 2007; Verster & Buning, 2000; Collège des médecins du Québec & Ordre des pharmaciens du Québec, 2000; Australian Department of Health and Ageing, 2003; nida, 1999a; U.K. Department of Health Scottish Office et al., 1999). Case managers also need to know about the potential risks and side effects of methadone use.

A good understanding of the prescribing and dosing aspects of mmt allows case managers to become active participants in treatment planning and collaborative decision making regarding issues such as dose adjustment and continuation on mmt, and to better address behavioural issues (Zweben, 1991; Kang et al., 1997).

When clients begin treatment, they may be overwhelmed by all the information they are provided with initially. They may also have picked up incomplete or inaccurate information from friends, the media or the Internet. They may not understand the regulations and protocols surrounding prescription, dosing, urine drug screening and other aspects of mmt, and they may have concerns or questions that need addressing. Case managers with a sound understanding of mmt principles can educate and reassure clients as well as direct them to their pharmacists and physicians for more in-depth information and discussion.

Case managers can also apply their knowledge to advocate on behalf of clients with any other health or social service providers with which their clients come into contact, and can educate providers of those services who also hold misconceptions about MMT (McCann et al., 1994).

Currently in Ontario, not all people who are acting in a case management function are required to learn about how methadone works in a formal, regulated or standardized way. There are many methadone-related courses, books and prescribing guidelines available, and many case managers and the agencies that employ them do seek out knowledge about methadone. But the extent to which they make these efforts, or succeed in becoming educated about methadone, is unknown.

Methadone is a regulated and controlled medication: its administration, prescribing and dosage protocols are governed by medical and legal guidelines, which affect many aspects of a client's experience in MMT. Currently, the College of Physicians and Surgeons of Ontario's *Methadone Maintenance Guidelines* (2005) provide the standardized document on the regulations and prescribing protocols of methadone maintenance in Ontario, and the Ontario College of Pharmacists provides dispensing policy. The better informed a case manager is about these policies, the more support, advocacy and assistance he or she can provide to clients.

A CLIENT TALKS ABOUT
KNOWLEDGE OF METHADONE

"[Case managers] should have a lot more knowledge about methadone and why people go on it. When they don't understand it feels judgmental. They should have more health knowledge and explain things better."

WHY DO CASE MANAGERS NEED TO KNOW ABOUT METHADONE AND MMT?

- Clients may need to review the basics of MMT so they can make informed choices. Physicians may have limited time to review information with clients or may not be immediately available when clients have questions.
- Clients may not understand the treatment protocols and processes. Case managers can help to correct any misinterpretations that may frustrate or worry a client and ultimately lead to treatment disengagement. For example, if a client says, "It takes so long to get my MMT dose at the pharmacy because the pharmacist doesn't like me," the case manager might suggest that the reason for the delay is more likely that it takes time to check and validate a prescription, especially if there is an error or a change in dose.
- Other members of the MMT team may make decisions about dosage levels, take-home doses, or dispensing that the client does not agree with. Knowing about MMT allows the case manager to participate in solving the problem and providing information and reassurance to the client.
- Understanding MMT allows case managers to be more alert to potential safety concerns (for example, recognizing that a client who is excessively drowsy may be at risk of overdose, or that unstable housing affects the ability to store take-home doses).
- Clients may feel more comfortable approaching case managers about issues, symptoms and concerns (such as "the pharmacist doesn't have a private place where I can ask her questions" or "the doctor is too busy"). The information that case managers provide is not a substitute for a dialogue between the client and the doctor or the pharmacist, but it can address immediate concerns. In fact, a skillful response by a case manager may encourage a client to communicate more effectively with the rest of the treatment team.
- Other agencies or third parties (for example, courts, probation services, child protection service or employers) may not understand how MMT works and may have questions or make decisions based on inaccurate knowledge. Being able to explain MMT in basic terms is an important part of advocacy.
- Understanding how MMT works allows case managers to spot errors or inconsistencies in the work of other members of the

treatment team. This awareness increases accountability, program safety and adherence to professional guidelines.
- Understanding how MMT works improves communication about case management with the rest of the treatment team and allows for integrated care.

EMPLOWERING CLIENTS

Effective communication can often prevent or resolve conflicts, but sometimes situations occur where clients may be deeply unsatisfied or concerned about the treatment they are receiving.

Although the specific procedures for clients to make complaints about treatment programs or a particular service provider are beyond the scope of this guide, some suggestions and discussion about this issue are important.

As active partners in their treatment, clients should be encouraged to first try to discuss their concerns and complaints at the program or provider level. Service providers should be open to feedback from clients and have clear mechanisms in place to deal with their complaints and concerns. The approach to resolving such concerns should be committed, prompt and sincere.

If the situation escalates beyond the program level, clients should be aware that various colleges govern the standards and conduct of professionals delivering services, and each one has a complaints procedure:
- The College of Physicians and Surgeons of Ontario
- The Ontario College of Nursing
- The Ontario College of Pharmacists
- The Ontario College of Social Workers and Social Service Workers
- The Office of the Ombudsman of Ontario

Information for clients about how to handle a disagreement or conflict with a service provider can be found in CAMH's *Methadone Maintenance Treatment: Client Handbook.*

PRACTICE POINT

PROVIDING ONGOING EDUCATION ABOUT MMT

Be prepared to educate clients and those involved with them (families, employers, social service providers, etc.) on an ongoing basis about various aspects of MMT.

MMT is a complex treatment; its unique dispensing and prescribing protocols, in place to ensure client and public safety, can be a challenge to understand. Hearing all of the information at once during client intake may not be enough—over time, clients and others connected with their treatment may need to have further education and review of why things work the way they do.

ORAL OPIOID USE

Fischer et al. (2008) found that, in Canada, people who have become dependent on oral opioids (whether supplies were obtained illegally from friends or drug dealers or legitimately through their own medical prescriptions) generally benefit from MMT, but may differ from injection heroin users in terms of their previous exposure to pain treatment or the presence of concurrent untreated mental health symptoms. More research and understanding about treatment approaches in light of these differences is needed (Fischer et al., 2006, 2008). Case managers need to be aware of the differences between these groups of clients, and should follow the emerging research and consider its implications for approaches to practice.

Programs that are specifically targeted to street-involved injection drug users may be a factor in the early drop-out rates of clients who do not identify with what has been historically the main client population for MMT and may still be perceived as such (Stevens et al., 2008). Research suggests that injection heroin use has become an increasingly marginal form of drug use among illegal opioid users in Canada and that Canada has one of the highest rates per capita for the consumption of prescription opioids, whether illegally obtained or prescribed for opioid-based pain treatment (Fischer et al., 2006).

PIERRE

SCENARIO: Pierre is a 60-year-old retired man with a 30-year history of oral opioid dependence and chronic pain issues. He has been on methadone for five months and is doing well. He meets with his case manager and tells him how uncomfortable he feels at the MMT clinic: "I never stuck a needle in my arm in my life. All I see here is pamphlets and posters about injecting. That's not me. I can't relate to any of these people. I don't want to come here any more."

REFLECTION: The case manager understands that not seeing his experience reflected in the other clients and in the educational material provided by the clinic may be a source of alienation for Pierre. It may also put him at risk for early treatment exit.

RESPONSE: The case manager acknowledges Pierre's negative feeling about the environment. He explores with Pierre his specific questions about oral opioid use and reassures him that while the clinic atmosphere and culture may not feel like a good fit, MMT is a good fit for opioid dependency. He points out that Pierre is actually doing well on methadone, and Pierre agrees. The case manager offers to investigate the possibility of having Pierre transfer his methadone care to a family-doctor-based practice, where the atmosphere and environment might be more comfortable for him than the methadone-only clinic.

PRACTICE POINT

REFLECTING THE EXPERIENCES OF ORAL OPIOID USERS

Ensure that educational materials supplied to clients address not only the risks of injecting or inhaling opioids but also the risks of oral opioid use. Be aware that some oral opioid users may find it difficult to engage in treatment if they perceive that the culture of the clinic or the knowledge of the workers is exclusively focused on injection users.

JOSEF

SCENARIO: Josef is a 45-year-old opioid-dependent client who has been on methadone for about eight months. He is doing well in the program and has now attained "level-2 carries" (that is, he can have two take-home doses a week). He has returned to work after two months off, during which his methadone dose was stabilized. He reports that things are going well at home with his wife and three teenage children. Josef and his wife want to know why Josef can't have extended "carries" so that he can take a long holiday with his family. Josef says he finds the program helpful but doesn't understand why "there are all these rules, all this control. . . . I would never abuse this medication and I don't know why the doctor can't trust me."

REFLECTION: The case manager understands that methadone is subject to a much more extensive set of guidelines and protocols than most other medications and that there are many regulations affecting how it is dispensed. She also knows that hearing all of this information at intake may be overwhelming for some clients and that they may not remember or understand quite how the system works. The case manager also wonders if there is another reason the doctor has been cautious about increasing Josef's level of take-home doses, and if there are other issues of concern from the doctor that Josef does not understand. She understands that, to promote integrated care, it is important for her to hear all of the information and concerns about take-home doses from both the client and the physician before advocating for a particular decision.

RESPONSE: The case manager reviews the dispensing and prescribing guidelines with Josef. She also suggests some strategies that would help him take his holiday, such as temporary guest dosing. The case manager offers to attend Josef's next doctor's appointment with him to discuss with the physician what needs to happen in order for Josef to work his way up to receiving more take-home doses. She also offers to meet with Josef and his wife to explain more about how methadone prescribing works.

SPLITTING

"Splitting" in the context of case management refers to a situation where a client, whether deliberately or inadvertently, behaves in a way that is potentially divisive to the treatment team: leaving out or altering information that has been conveyed by one member of the team and then seeking to engage the advocacy of another team member for help.

In any situation where a problem or potential problem with another team member is stated or implied, the case manager should be sure to obtain an objective and factual account of what was said and done and why decisions were made before committing to client advocacy. It is important to respond to the client's distress and anxiety with empathy and reassurance, but not to jump to conclusions before understanding the complete story.

Following any such incident, it can be helpful to meet with the client and the other team member together to ensure that any issues are clarified and that communication is consistent.

COUNSELLING SKILLS AND APPROACHES

The panel recommends that:

15. Case managers receive training and develop skills in motivational interviewing, structured relapse prevention counselling and cognitive-behavioural therapy. [III]

A case manager requires counselling skills in order to:

- help clients identify and make the changes they want in regards to their use of substances
- encourage clients to engage with other potentially beneficial services (for example, employment programs and parenting classes)
- assist clients to make lifestyle changes (for example, improving nutrition, positive use of leisure time)
- help clients cope with any psychological and social barriers they may face (for example, internalized guilt, shame, exclusion from family or relationship supports, low self-esteem).

Assisting clients to make changes and break old patterns so that they can more fully benefit from the stability that MMT offers is more effective when evidence-based approaches are used.

Many studies examining counselling modalities, both in general substance use populations and in MMT populations, identify motivational interviewing, structured relapse prevention and cognitive-behavioural therapies as best practice models that improve outcomes and increase treatment retention levels (Dzialdowski et al., 1998; Brown & Dongier, 2005; Ball et al., 2007; Rollnick et al., 2008; Health Canada, 1999; DiClemente & Velasquez, 2002). For more refractory and unstable clients, outreach and targeted risk reduction strategies have shown positive potential for treatment retention (Booth et al., 2004; CSAT, 2005).

MOTIVATIONAL INTERVIEWING

Motivational interviewing is a communication and client/counsellor partnership approach that focuses on enhancing clients' motivation by exploring and resolving their ambivalence.

Motivational interviewing assumes a collaborative approach rather than a confrontational one. The client's perspectives, feelings and expertise about his or her own situation are incorporated into a dialogue with the counsellor. Issues of ambivalence about change are explored together, and the client's autonomy to make decisions about behaviour is respected. The four keys to motivational interviewing are:
- empathic listening and reflection
- exploring discrepancy
- rolling with resistance
- supporting self-efficacy.

STRUCTURED RELAPSE PREVENTION

Structured relapse prevention is a counselling approach that focuses on a client's ability to make changes in his or her substance use. The counsellor works with the client to explore concrete, practical skills and techniques, for example:
- managing cravings
- coping with high-risk situations
- developing alternative coping skills
- planning what to do if a slip occurs.

COGNITIVE-BEHAVIOURAL THERAPY

Cognitive-behavioural therapy helps a client explore the connection between what he or she thinks and how he or she behaves. It is often offered as a brief, solution-focused course of treatment.

PRACTICE POINT

COUNSELLING

- Be aware that clients' responses to counselling may vary according to their personal perspectives on making changes. Some may prefer more structured and prescriptive approaches, while others may struggle with ambivalence and place a high value on self-determination. Others will move back and forth between feeling motivated to change and feeling unconcerned about current behaviours. The wider your range of techniques and skills, the better equipped you will be to find an approach that fits well with your clients' own personal style, thereby facilitating their behavioural change.
- Work to improve your counselling skills through courses, text materials, hands-on workshops and clinical supervision. Over time, practice, reflection and self-evaluation will lead to the development of a genuine, personalized communication and counselling style.

CLIENTS TALK ABOUT
COUNSELLING APPROACHES

"[Case managers and other service providers need] better training about what it's like to be addicted. Better understanding. 'Stop, don't do it' doesn't work."

"Case managers should show respect and not judge clients. Sometimes they don't care how we feel and what we are going through."

"They [case managers] need to listen more to what we want, not just what they think is good for us."

"Help clients make changes—push them forward."

"Help me not relapse. Support is helpful. Make it easy to get to."

"Be friendly, open, non-judgmental. Make it easy for people to connect with counselling services."

"[My case managers] don't push it, they let it work itself out. They don't criticize. They listen. They are always here for me. This program saved my life."

URINE DRUG SCREENING
The panel recommends that:
16. Case managers understand the basic science behind, and the limitations of, urine drug screening and have the ability to clearly explain, to clients and to providers of other social and community services, the issues surrounding the use of urine drug screening and the usefulness of the results in terms of measuring overall client progress. [IV]

Ongoing monitoring of clients' substance use is a component of MMT and usually involves urine drug screening for methadone, methadone metabolite, other opioids and other potentially harmful substances such as benzodiazepines and cocaine.

Urine drug screening is done for a number of reasons:
- as part of the medical assessment, to diagnose opioid dependence
- to confirm clients' reports of drug use and to inform treatment decisions
- to confirm consumption of take-home doses
- to identify possible safety concerns that can arise when clients are not taking their dose as prescribed or are taking drugs that are associated with increased medical risk for people on MMT
- to provide clients with a concrete and tangible record of their positive achievements in maintaining reduced drug use (if that is their goal)

The frequency of urine drug screening (which is typically conducted randomly) is determined by the client's length of time in treatment and stability. Many physicians or clinics, or both, require that the client be observed while providing the sample, or that the authenticity of the sample be otherwise verified.

Urine drug screening, while helpful in determining substance use, has many limitations. It cannot with accuracy determine the amount of any substance used, the time of use or the level of impairment resulting from use. Representatives of social service or other third-party agencies (for example, probation officers and child protection workers) who request information about urine screen results from a case manager need to understand the limitations on using urine drug screen information to make clinical or sanctioning decisions. Case managers, because they are often the liaison and advocate for the client, need to have a full understanding of the rationale and science behind urine drug screens and to be able to explain these to other agencies.

Case managers also need to be able to explain the rationale and science behind urine drug screening to clients, who may have questions about the use of and need for screens, and may find the requirement of providing a sample under supervision stressful, anxiety-provoking and even degrading. Case managers need to be able to address these concerns by providing clients with coping skills and reassurance.

KEESHA

SCENARIO: Keesha is a 28-year-old MMT client. She has been doing well on methadone for the past two years, with occasional use of opioids every few months. Keesha meets with her counsellor regularly and is working hard at identifying her triggers. She says that it's tempting to use when she sees her friends, but she's avoiding being with them and has gone from using with them every weekend to using with them every two months.

She brings a letter to the case manager from her probation officer. The officer has requested to have a copy of Keesha's urine drug screening results so that he can validate that she is doing well in treatment and make decisions about her compliance with probation orders. Keesha has given her consent.

REFLECTION: The case manager understands that urine drug screening results are not the sole indicator of a client's progress in treatment. She also knows they cannot accurately or reliably tell how much of the substance was used, and that they occasionally show false positives. The case manager recognizes that while urine drug screening is a helpful indicator, there are limitations to what it can predict or evaluate in terms of how the client is doing. She realizes that some professionals in community or government agencies may not understand these limitations or know how to comprehensively evaluate a client's progress.

RESPONSE: With Keesha's permission, the case manager contacts the probation officer to discuss the limits of information that urine drug screening can provide. She explains that the results are only part of the larger picture, which overall indicates improvement. Keesha's attendance at appointments, regular involvement in counselling, stable housing and vocational pursuits are all measures of progress. The probation officer agrees to take these factors into account when evaluating Keesha's compliance.

PRACTICE POINT

ISSUES WITH URINE DRUG SCREENING

- Be prepared to educate both clients and providers of health and social services about the role of urine drug screening, making clear that drug screen results by themselves do not paint an accurate picture of client progress but must be seen as one part of a bigger picture.
- Note that some clients may experience stress and anxiety when requested to provide urine samples under observation. Talk with clients about things they can do to cope better, such as relaxation and breathing exercises, positive self-talk and practising voiding "on command." Be alert to clients who express undue levels of anxiety—their anxiety may be an indicator that they are experiencing triggers related to sexual or physical past trauma.

CLIENTS TALK ABOUT
URINE DRUG SCREENING

"[Case management has been helpful] because of setting short-term goals, like staying clean for the next two weeks. It helps having someone watching me and checking in with me and urine screens are part of that too."

"You need to be here for urine samples but frequently staff are on a break and it makes it difficult to wait when you have to pee. They sometimes close 10 minutes early, which makes it difficult to get here with work hours' restrictions."

"There are no longer urine screening collection services in town X, where I used to live, so I would have no carries unless I travelled here [town Y] once a week, but I couldn't afford that. So I decided to come to town Y to be closer. There is a urine screening facility in town Z but you have to do it on command. If you can't, then you are out of luck. It's a $50 cab ride from where I live. Here, I can try and pee several times if I need to, so I decided to come here."

"See beyond the drug use and health problems. See me as a person, the things I am doing, like going to school."

POLYSUBSTANCE USE

The panel recommends that:

17. Case managers know the risks of polysubstance use and the health teaching issues surrounding polysubstance use, and apply this knowledge to their assessment of, engagement with and referral of clients with polysubtance use. [III]

Clients who are polysubstance users derive benefit from MMT in terms of reduced substance use and treatment retention. These benefits are increased when clients are offered specific, targeted substance use counselling, enhanced outreach and treatment engagement. Generally, polysubstance use while in MMT puts clients at high risk for dropping out of treatment (Joe et al., 2001; Magura et al., 2002; Woody et al., 1995; Rosenblum et al., 1995; Booth et al., 2004; CSAT, 2005).

Case managers should understand the basics of the interaction of other substances with methadone (information usually provided in a basic course on the pharmacology of methadone). This is important because polysubstance use can:

- make it difficult to determine if a client's dose of methadone is too low or too high, as symptoms of either condition may be masked or altered by the presence of additional substances
- mask or exacerbate symptoms of anxiety or depression or other mental health issues, making diagnosis and treatment difficult
- place a client at serious medical risk (for example, if alcohol or benzo-diazepines are used in conjunction with methadone)
- impair a client's ability to learn new coping strategies and behaviours in response to stress, triggers and drug use situations.

Case managers also need to be able to explain to clients the issues and concerns related to polysubstance use.

HARM REDUCTION

Harm reduction focuses on reducing the harm of drug use for the user and to society, rather than requiring abstinence as a condition of treatment. Harm reduction and low-threshold MMT programs that provide basic services to marginalized and difficult-to-engage clients show promising results in terms of reducing high-risk behaviours such as injecting, needle sharing, unsafe sex and criminality (Johnson et al., 2001; Csete, 2007; BC MOH, 2005; Phillips & Rosenberg, 2008).

People who are dependent on opioids and continue to use these and other substances risk overdose. Research suggests that most of these overdoses are reported by clients as accidental overdoses rather than deliberate suicide attempts. Educating clients about overdose issues in order to reduce the risk is considered an appropriate intervention (Kosten & Rounsaville, 1988; Darke & Ross, 2001).

Health teaching is an important component of harm reduction. In the context of MMT, this involves educating clients about behaviours that will reduce the risk of serious medical consequences related to drug use and to unprotected sex. It helps the user to reduce some of the risks associated with drug use without requiring that all drug use be stopped, sending a message of respect and understanding for the user's immediate needs (Rosenbaum, 1997; Martin et al., 2003; Health Canada, 2002a). Clients can receive health teaching from any member of the MMT team, but given time or other constraints of the contact with some of the team members (for example, it may be difficult for a pharmacist to speak confidentially with a patient in a busy pharmacy), case managers are often in the best position to provide this service.

PROTECTION AND EDUCATION*

The panel recommends that:

18. Case managers have knowledge of harm reduction practices, including safer injection, safer sex and overdose protection, and educate their clients about these practices and issues. [III]

19. Case managers ensure that clients have easy and ready access to health education and harm reduction materials and supplies, such as informational literature, condoms and injection and inhalation supplies. [IV]

---

* Much of the following section on harm reduction has been adapted with permission from the authors and publishers of the Ontario Needle Exchange's best practice recommendations on needle exchange programs (Strike et al., 2006). Those guidelines for best practice are applicable to MMT case managers working with clients who are injection drug users.

People using opioids, particularly those who inject or who engage in high-risk behaviours such as needle sharing and unprotected sex, are at risk of:
- contracting or infecting others with sexually transmitted diseases, HIV and hepatitis C
- developing serious medical conditions, such as abscesses and infections
- overdosing.

By talking with clients about how to reduce the risks, providing them with access to harm reduction materials (such as sterile injection equipment and condoms) and educating them about proper self-care (such as safer injection strategies and vein care), Strike et al. (2006) found needle exchange workers can greatly assist in reducing the harms that these conditions cause; it seems reasonable to extrapolate that case managers in MMT can achieve similar results through these actions.

While providing written informational material to injection drug users or clients engaging in high-risk practices may be of some benefit to those clients who can read it, simply having and reading these materials does not necessarily effect change in the clients' behaviour. Case managers need to be aware of the forces and triggers that influence clients to engage in high-risk behaviour and to use other educational and harm reduction strategies to address these factors.

Research reviewed by Strike et al. (2006) suggests that "injection behaviours are typically learned from and reinforced by peer groups"— that is, clients may learn unsafe techniques from another user and then continue to use these practices despite the availability of alternative and safer techniques. Strike et al. (2006) write that Paone et al. (1997) "have noted that attempts to change individual injection behaviours may be difficult if injection norms within social networks favour unsafe behaviours."

Demonstrating safer injection techniques (Hawkins et al., 1999 [as cited in Strike et al., 2006]) and using computer-assisted education (Marsch & Bickel, 2004 [as cited in Strike et al.]) are interventions that have resulted in delivering greater behavioural change than just providing access to equipment. As well, research suggests (Morrison et al., 1997 [as cited in Strike]) that injection drug users are often reluctant to seek medical treatment for injection-related problems until they reach a crisis point.

Proactively encouraging clients to seek medical assistance before problems escalate is viewed as a helpful strategy for needle exchange program workers; again, we can extrapolate that, since case managers are very much in the same position relative to clients as needle exchange program workers, they may be able to provide clients with harm reduction supplies, explore questions, concerns and myths about high-risk behaviours and encourage contact with medical and health services in a timely manner.

Overdose is also an ongoing concern, particularly for clients who cycle in and out of methadone treatment. Since tolerance to opioids decreases rapidly when use is reduced or stopped, clients who miss their dose for more than three days are at increased risk for overdose if they then use amounts of opioids at levels for which they no longer have a tolerance (CPSO, 2005). Missed doses can occur, for example, when a client is unexpectedly hospitalized or incarcerated and not provided with methadone while in care or custody, or when a client leaves care or custody and there is a delay in continuing methadone in the community due to gaps in prescription coverage. As another example, if a client diverts take-home methadone (either by selling or giving away some or all of it to someone else), that dose is reduced or missed entirely, and consequently over a short period of time he or she loses tolerance for the dose prescribed. If the client then suddenly receives the usual full or original dose (as might happen if the client has to take the dose under observation during a hospital admission or because of a loss of carry privileges), the client risks overdosing.

By following the best practices of maintaining contact with clients on a regular basis and of becoming knowledgeable about the pharmacology of methadone, including the risk factors associated with and relationships among reductions in methadone dose, changes in tolerance and the potential for overdose, case managers are well positioned to educate clients about the dangers of diverting methadone or not taking it exactly as prescribed, and about what to do if they miss several doses.

The role of the case manager parallels that of the needle exchange worker in that both work to help clients reduce harm and seek appropriate medical attention and preventive care. While expert medical and pharmacological advice and guidance are the best ways for clients to reduce their risks, it is often not practical for clients to approach their doctors and pharmacists directly with questions and concerns: the setting, such as a pharmacy, may not provide adequate privacy, or an appointment with a physician may be too brief to allow or encourage this discussion. In addition, the client may be reluctant to disclose difficulties because of shame, stigmatization or a lack of trust in medical professionals.

The panel found no direct evidence regarding the impact, positive or negative, of case managers being the distributors of supplies such as needles and condoms directly to clients. Panel members' experience suggests that not all clients feel comfortable asking a case manager for injection or inhalation supplies or for large quantities of condoms; clients may fear that because such requests suggest they are using injection drugs or working in the sex trade, they may perceive that it will lead to the case manager reporting this information to other parties, such as a child protection agency. Nonetheless, the panel concluded that it is important to give clients the option to access harm reduction supplies, either through a case manager or through another health or community service provider.

Education and awareness related to sharing needles and safe sex are ongoing issues that should be revisited with clients on a regular basis. Frequent contact, risk reduction reinforcement, empathic support in the case of relapse to high-risk behaviours and prevention advocacy have been identified as effective interventions for refractory injection drug users (Booth et al., 2004).

NICOLE

SCENARIO: Nicole is a 28-year-old injection drug user who has been on methadone for about one year. She has improved her attendance at the clinic and rarely misses a dose. Her urine drug screening results consistently show positive for opioids and Nicole states that she does inject, although "not as often as before." In her infrequent contacts with the case manager she is pleasant but guarded, responding to most questions by saying, "Everything is fine, I'm just not ready to stop yet."

REFLECTION: The case manager recognizes that clients with high-risk behaviours may benefit from information and education to reduce the harms of using, particularly when the information comes from a peer. The case manager also recognizes that some clients may be reluctant to ask for information or harm reduction supplies because they feel embarrassed or ashamed, or worry that admitting to high-risk use will affect how their care providers view them. The case manager also recognizes that some clients have had negative encounters with health care providers in the past, which may prevent them from talking about their high-risk behaviours.

RESPONSE: The case manager provides baskets of condoms and dental dams in innocuous locations where clients can help themselves. The case manager ensures that there are posters and pamphlets available about safer injecting, overdose and safer sex at an appropriate literacy level (written plainly, featuring many clear illustrations and presented in different languages as appropriate to the community). The case manager also posts information about sources for clean needles and supplies, anonymous testing, peer support and other community harm reduction resources.

The case manager also checks in regularly with Nicole about any health concerns or questions she may have and invites her to ask questions or talk about these concerns.

CLIENTS TALK ABOUT
HARM REDUCTION

"It's hard to trust anybody after years of use. Sometimes you don't want to answer their questions honestly because you are not sure how it will affect your methadone. More so at the beginning."

"Harm reduction, health teaching and needle exchange—back when I was using this really helped a lot."

"Be easy to approach. [Case managers] need to be able to gain our trust."

PRACTICE POINT

TEACHING HARM REDUCTION

- While clients benefit from harm reduction education, they may be reluctant to seek it out because of past negative experiences or personal issues of shame and embarrassment. Invite questions or discussion on the topic, and make information available in a variety of ways (for example, through posters, pamphlets, informal health teaching groups, community peer educators, etc.).
- Provide easily accessible supplies along with clear and understandable ways to use them. If harm reduction support is not available onsite, offer to connect clients with support opportunities in the community.
- Keep up to date on harm reduction issues, staying current with emerging scientific findings and research about transmission and protection concerns.

The panel recommends that:

20. Case managers receive specialized training about the transmission and progression of infection and the psychosocial issues surrounding HIV and hepatitis C. [III]

21. Case managers know about, and liaise with, community resources that can provide services and supports to clients infected with HIV or hepatitis C, and to partners and families. [IV]

22. Case managers assist with, and advocate for, the co-ordination and provision of medical care for clients with HIV or hepatitis C infection. [IV]

MMT clients with HIV or hepatitis C infection need to co-ordinate their primary medical care with their methadone treatment. Certain medications used to treat these infections may have an impact on the way methadone is metabolized, and both the client and the primary care physician need to be aware of possible adverse interactions (CPSO, 2005; Health Canada, 2002a). This group of clients may also benefit from other services such as specialized support groups, nutrition programs, food banks and additional financial assistance (so that the client can afford nutritious food) (Health Canada, 2002a; CSAT, 2005; Dennis et al., 1992; Ball & Ross, 1991; Strike et al., 2006).

CLIENTS TALK ABOUT
HIV AND HEPATITIS C

"I found out I was hep C positive when I started MMT. There was no one here to help me with the fallout. It was devastating. When they asked me if I would consent to be tested for HIV, I said no. I felt there would be no net for me. They don't give you follow-up."

"It's hard to have restrictive carries, one week at a time. It impedes my health care for HIV. It's stressful to travel so far to get my methadone."

PRACTICE POINT

SUPPORTING CLIENTS WITH HIV OR HEPATITIS C INFECTION

- Facilitate access to primary care treatment for HIV and hepatitis C infection. Ensure that all members of the MMT and primary medical care teams co-ordinate treatment and communicate about any issues and concerns. As needed, help clients with HIV or hepatitis C infection to access community resources

that provide services (counselling, financial assistance, peer support, etc.).
- Be prepared to support clients with related issues, from transmission and disease progression, to relationship and family concerns, to dealing with stigma.

The panel recommends that:

23. Because it has been shown that clients who receive outreach and counselling are more likely to re-engage in addiction treatment programs than those who do not receive it [Ib], programs and case managers ensure that clients who drop out of MMT during the early stages of treatment have opportunities to receive ongoing supportive outreach and to resume treatment. [III]

Clients who drop out of MMT are more likely to re-engage in treatment if there is an effort made to keep in touch with them through some form of outreach, ranging from telephone contact and informal community visiting, to access through drop-in programs that offer practical support, harm reduction education and materials, and supportive counselling and case management (Goldstein et al., 2002).

STAYING IN TREATMENT

Clients who drop out of methadone treatment early and go back to high-risk opioid use have greater rates of mortality. The single biggest predictor of improved treatment outcome is treatment retention.

JANA

SCENARIO: Jana is a 26-year-old street-involved opioid injection drug user. She frequently drops in to see her case manager for help with practical things like filling out forms, referrals to food banks or shelters, and bus tokens. Jana does not reveal much about her personal feelings and issues, but says that she looks forward to "saying hi" to her case manager whenever they run into each other at the agency. Jana frequently misses her doctor's appointments and urine drug screening appointments, and about six months into her MMT she does not show up at the clinic for a week. When her case manager contacts her by phone, Jana says that she is fine but has decided that methadone isn't for her and that she won't be coming back to the clinic.

REFLECTION: The case manager understands that an early treatment exit will greatly increase the risk of Jana's continuing to engage in high-risk behaviours, put her health at greater risk and lead to greater social instability. The case manager also understands that clients who drop out of treatment can be encouraged to re-engage with treatment if they are offered supportive outreach.

RESPONSE: The case manager encourages Jana to keep in touch and suggests she call or contact the clinic regularly to talk about how things are going for her. The case manager also gives Jana information and phone numbers for drop-in and front-line services that can provide her with food, shelter and access to health care and clean injection equipment.

CLIENTS TALK
ABOUT OUTREACH

"Be a good listener and good communicator. It's important to be available when needed. Even when I moved to another program in another city, it was important for me to be able to check in with my counsellor from time to time."

"Follow-up and outreach. If you leave the program maybe they could follow up with you to see if you really want to quit and give you a chance to change your mind."

"I would like to have case management but I always procrastinate. It's probably a good idea but I don't follow through with things. I go to agency M once or twice a month to get food and to attend their drop-in."

PRACTICE POINT

CLIENTS WHO LEAVE TREATMENT EARLY

Recognize that many clients are ambivalent about changing their use. If a client leaves treatment early:
- keep the door open for an eventual return to treatment
- encourage him or her to use resources that will provide practical supportive assistance and reduce harms, such as needle exchanges and drop-in health services
- where possible, provide ongoing case management and counselling services as needed, or provide referrals to services that can
- stress that leaving treatment does not make someone a "failure"—point out that he or she may not be ready at this time for this type of treatment
- explore with the client what might help him or her reconnect with treatment.

CONFIDENTIALITY AND INFORMATION SHARING

The panel recommends that:

24. Case managers have a demonstrated understanding of the laws and policies that govern the disclosure of information about a client, and operate in accordance with these laws and policies. [IV]

25. Case managers play a role in educating clients about the issues surrounding consent and information sharing. Working with other members of the MMT care team, they ensure that clients understand what information must, by law, be reported to external agencies; how sharing information among members of the MMT care team is beneficial; what their rights are regarding consent for information sharing; and what the implications are of sharing information with external services and third parties (such as employers). Case managers discuss these issues with the client when treatment begins. [IV]

Sharing information about a client's drug use, stability and overall progress can be a helpful adjunct to treatment.

Within the immediate circle of care (i.e., the prescribing physician, the pharmacist, other clinic staff or program workers), sharing information can clarify treatment issues and allow for timely intervention if necessary. This kind of communication is called for in many clinical treatment guides and recommendations. Clients should be made aware of the benefits of such information sharing and their consent to it should be sought (Ridgely & Willenbring, 1992; SSAM, 2007; Australian Department of Health and Ageing, 2003; CSAT, 2005; CPSO, 2005).

Responding to requests for information about clients from external agencies (such as driver's licensing authorities, social service agencies, child protection services and justice systems) may also contribute to integrated and co-ordinated treatment, but should be handled with care and discretion by case managers. Professional protocols for the release of information, as well as other professional obligations, such as the duty to inform and child protection regulations, are clearly detailed in Ontario's Regulated Health Professionals Act and by professional regulatory bodies (e.g., the Ontario College of Social Workers and Social Service Workers and the Ontario College of Nursing). In addition, if a case manager is performing duties for a particular social service agency, that agency's governing and accountability guidelines will influence the case manager's actions.

Knowing the boundaries, legal frameworks and clinical guidelines that pertain to the practice of one's profession is typically a standard practice requirement for regulated health professionals. Some case managers are members of regulated professions; others are governed by agency guidelines. Whatever a case manager's background, having a good understanding of the ethical, legal and clinical issues relating to sharing client information will allow the case manager to respond ethically and professionally to requests for such sharing.

JIM

SCENARIO: Jim, a 45-year-old oral opioid user, is beginning methadone treatment. Jim meets with the case manager at assessment and is very open and candid about his difficulties with his opioid use and his relationship with his family. Toward the end of the interview he asks, "Who else is going to know my business here? Do the doctor and the pharmacist need to know what we talk about? I'd rather keep all of that information separate."

REFLECTION: The case manager understands that open communication with the team about client progress and issues in treatment improves co-ordination and leads to better outcomes. He knows what kinds of information need to be shared with the team (urgent care concerns and any information directly relevant to treatment decisions and issues) and what is discretionary (details of the counselling sessions). He is well informed about the legal and agency requirements regarding content in clinical note-taking. The case manager also understands that client concerns about confidentiality and discretion are important and should be taken into account when making decisions about sharing information.

Continued on page 103

Continued from page 102

RESPONSE: The case manager explains to Jim why shared information can help his care: for example, if the pharmacist notices that Jim is on another medication for other health problems that might interact negatively with his methadone, the pharmacist needs to be able to contact the doctor with this concern. Similarly, if the case manager notices that Jim seems very depressed or has many complaints of vague symptoms, then communicating this knowledge to the doctor may be helpful in managing Jim's care. If the concern is of an urgent nature (for example, if there is risk of suicide or homicide or endangerment of a child, or if the information is requested by a court order), then reporting is mandatory.

The case manager makes clear to Jim that he will be informed of requests to share information from outside sources, and he will have the option of providing written permission or refusal for these requests. The case manager emphasizes that MMT works best when all care providers can share information that will improve treatment outcome.

CLIENTS TALK ABOUT
INFORMATION SHARING

"Confidentiality is important. You have to take your drink with so many other people. I don't want my employer to know."

"There has been a lack of care and communication and confusion with my HIV meds. The methadone wasn't holding me due to medication interactions."

"I felt sick for weeks and didn't know it was because my dose was too high."

PRACTICE POINT

CLIENT CONFIDENTIALITY

- Sharing information with the methadone care team improves care. Confidentiality and sharing of information must take into account the client's consent, mandatory reporting obligations, agency mandates and regulated professional requirements. Be familiar with these boundaries, be able to explain them to clients and seek supervision when in doubt.
- Understand client concerns and experiences with confidentiality and be prepared to support, acknowledge and problem-solve.

CONCURRENT DISORDERS

The panel recommends that:

26. Case managers demonstrate knowledge of the complex connections between mental health and substance use. [III]

27. Case managers understand the assessment components for concurrent disorders and be able to refer clients to mental health service agencies and/or agencies that treat concurrent disorders. They use collaborative treatment planning strategies to ensure that MMT clients with concurrent disorders receive cohesive and co-ordinated treatment. [IV]

28. Case managers have a demonstrated knowledge of assessment and intervention for suicidality, de-escalation and crisis response. [IV]

Case managers need to understand the complex relationship between mental health disorders and substance use. It is common for opioid-dependent people to have mental health problems, but it can be difficult to distinguish symptoms related to the mental health problems from those related to substance use.

People who are opioid dependent have high rates of suicide and attempted suicide (and also of accidental overdose; see the "Harm reduction" section above), and the rates are even higher among those with concurrent disorders and psychosocial dysfunction (Krausz et al., 1996; Chatham et al., 1995).

All clinicians, intake workers and case managers working with people who are opioid dependent should be able to recognize risk factors and warning signs and be able to assess, intervene appropriately and make referrals for suicidal and homicidal clients (CSAT, 2005).

Clients with a diagnosis of antisocial personality disorder and polysubstance use tend to have poorer outcomes in MMT and have a higher risk of treatment dropout. This category of MMT client is often described as "difficult to treat." No single treatment approach for this population has been demonstrated as significantly superior over others (Rounsaville et al., 1982; Darke et al., 1994; Alterman & Cacciola, 1991; Havens & Strathdee, 2005).

Clients with other types of concurrent disorders require more intensive case management and specifically targeted counselling in addition to MMT, but do well when these supports are provided (Van den Bosch & Verheul, 2007; Saxon et al., 1994; Gossop, Marsden et al., 2006). The combination of substance use and concurrent mental health disorders is recognized as a challenging diagnostic and treatment issue (Schuckit & Hasselbrock, 1994; Skinner, 2005; Health Canada, 2002b). The mental health needs of substance users often go unmet (Darke et al., 1994). However, failure to provide appropriate diagnosis and treatment for mental health disorders in substance users leads to poorer outcomes (McLellan et al., 1983; Scott et al., 1998). Scott et al. (1998) recommend enhanced training for mental health and substance use treatment providers in recognizing and treating concurrent disorders.

Social determinants of health, such as housing, income and social support networks, can greatly affect a person's mental health. Case managers should therefore incorporate considerations of these determinants into their assessment and treatment planning for MMT clients with concurrent disorders (Hawkings & Gilburt, 2004).

To provide comprehensive service to clients with concurrent disorders the case manager should have an understanding of:
- the prevalence of and interaction between substance use and mental health
- mental health disorders, including anxiety, depression, posttraumatic stress disorder, antisocial personality disorder, borderline personality

disorder, schizophrenia and bipolar disorders, eating disorders, self-harming behaviours

- identification, screening and assessment tools and strategies
- referral to concurrent disorder care or, in communities where this service is not available, advocacy for integrated and co-ordinated care between existing mental health services and MMT.

A diagnosis of mental health problems may be clouded by the presence of an active substance dependency, so comprehensive treatment for both issues may be delayed (Health Canada, 2002b). Often, clients may have lived highly unstable and chaotic lives for many years, which may have created substantial problems surrounding their housing, overall physical health and social supports. These clients may face more challenges in terms of becoming stable in many areas of their lives, and may have reduced capabilities to make and maintain the needed changes. Case managers should provide extra support and co-ordination of services to ensure that basic needs such as food, housing, financial supports and access to primary medical care are met for this group.

Some mental health problems are of a chronic and relapsing nature, similar to substance use. Some clients will cycle in and out of periods of mental illness such that when their psychiatric symptoms flare up their substance use may increase, and vice versa. MMT service providers should make efforts to accommodate unstable behaviours, missed appointments and missed doses in the recognition that clients displaying increased symptoms (more drug use, more mental health problems) need to have *increased* support—not to be discharged for non-compliance. Case managers should act as advocates and supporters for clients who are experiencing problems with program compliance.

PRACTICE POINT

CLIENTS WITH MENTAL HEALTH PROBLEMS

- Monitor and discuss with clients any significant changes in their mood (especially depression and anxiety) and coping patterns, and encourage communication with the physician about these changes. Clients may have been using opioids to control or self-medicate their psychiatric symptoms. When they reduce their use of opioids and begin MMT, their symptoms may become more prominent.
- When mental health services are providing psychiatric medication and monitoring to a client on MMT, encourage open communication among the various care providers, including pharmacists, psychiatrists and physicians. Be aware that some medications used in the treatment of mental health problems are contraindicated or interact negatively with methadone.
- Realize that clients with mental health problems may already have demands placed on them by their mental health needs (such as many appointments with different care providers and the taking of multiple medications). They may find the additional demands of MMT challenging. Work with clients to increase their time management skills and ability to cope with complex systems of care.

TANYA

SCENARIO: Tanya is a 40-year-old injection drug user who has been off and on methadone treatment for the past 10 years.

She often states that she is too anxious to leave her home and has a pattern of missing her dose and her appointments, then restarting her medication. Tanya tells her case manager that she saw a psychiatrist years ago, but "she didn't really help me and the medication she put me on made me feel tired all the time, so I stopped."

Tanya has again missed several days of her dose, and when the case manager contacts her by phone, Tanya tells him that she is too anxious and depressed to even think about going through the whole process of starting methadone again. She says that she really thinks it's useless for her to keep on trying.

REFLECTION: The case manager knows that opioid-dependent people often have untreated or undiagnosed mental health problems and that addressing both substance use and mental health problems is best practice. He understands that Tanya's concurrent depression and anxiety may place her at risk for suicide.

RESPONSE: The case manager convinces Tanya to come in to see him the next day and makes a plan with her to call the distress hotline should she feel unable to cope for the next 24 hours. He discusses with her the possibility of being referred to mental health services for evaluation and ongoing treatment. When Tanya comes in to see him, the case manager initiates a referral for community mental health services. As the wait-list for services is extensive, the case manager works with Tanya to come up with a safety plan and provides her with crisis numbers she can call if her depression and anxiety get worse.

The case manager also alerts Tanya's methadone prescriber. The case manager offers to escort Tanya to her appointment with her family doctor in order to discuss her symptoms and to talk about the option of medication to assist her until she can be seen at mental health services.

PRACTICE POINT

WORKING WITH CONCURRENT DISORDERS

- Ensure that any mental health concerns about a client are communicated to the whole MMT team.
- Refer clients to mental health care providers as appropriate. If the needed care is not readily available or there are wait-lists, put strategies in place to support the client in the meantime.
- Educate clients about the interplay between mental health and substance use.
- Make a safety plan with the client about how to handle a crisis: whom to call, what to do, where to go, etc.
- Teach the client self-soothing and emotional regulation techniques, and how to self-monitor and reach out before a problem becomes overwhelming.
- Collaborate with other health and community services to support the client's interactions with multiple service systems. Be prepared to advocate for care for the client and to educate mental health providers about the benefits of treating both addiction and mental health problems concurrently for improving client stability and treatment outcomes.

CLIENTS TALK ABOUT
MENTAL HEALTH

"I'm on benzos prescribed by my psychiatrist for anxiety, so I don't get any carries. This has increased my anxiety because it conflicts with school. I have an 8:00 a.m. start (the pharmacy is closed then), so I have to wait until after classes to get my methadone. I'm anxious all day."

"The MMT program referred me to a mental health and addictions worker at W hospital. It worked out great."

"Have counsellors available. Train them to deal with you when you are emotional."

> *"Case managers need to know more about mental health and how to help you with these issues. They need to take the time to get to know you. I'm shy about reaching out."*
>
> *"If I have a problem, I can call my case manager and she will look for ways to help me. It makes me feel good. I have to get the courage to call. When I do, I feel better—a big load of stress leaves me."*

TRAUMA

The panel recommends that:

29. Case managers receive basic training in issues of trauma and post-traumatic stress disorder. They have basic skills in handling disclosure, emotional disregulation, escalation and crisis response. [IV]

30. Case managers be aware of the limitations of their own expertise and training and not address trauma issues in an in-depth way unless they have been properly trained to do so and have adequate agency and supervisory support. [IV]

Trauma and sexual abuse histories are not unique to women, but women report higher incidences of these experiences.

People who use substances have higher rates of trauma histories than the general population, and higher rates of posttraumatic stress disorder. These conditions are often under-diagnosed and under-treated. The provision of counselling and support services targeting these issues increases treatment retention and decreases substance use. It is particularly important to include questions about trauma history and experience in a client's initial psychosocial assessment and to formulate engagement and treatment strategies to address these issues (Schiff et al., 2002; CSAT, 2005; Harrison & Carver, 2004).

PRACTICE PERSPECTIVE

"It's overwhelming sometimes. They come in crying, talking about flashbacks and abuse they had as kids, and I just don't know what to do. I don't have time to sit with them and listen to them, because I'm run off my feet here with all the other clients, and the phone is always ringing and I'm trying to sort out prescriptions. And the wait-list for special counselling services that deal with this kind of thing is very long. It breaks my heart and I feel so bad that I can't help. . . ."
—Case manager at methadone clinic, employed seven years

CLIENT CONSULTATION FINDINGS

TRAUMA AND ABUSE

- Over 70% of the clients surveyed stated that they thought it was extremely important that case managers be able to provide counselling and support for trauma and abuse issues.
- Over half of the clients surveyed stated that they occasionally sought help from case managers or counsellors about trauma or abuse issues.

PRACTICE POINT

TRAUMA

- Understand that many clients will have histories of trauma and abuse. Incorporate trauma-informed approaches to treatment into the agency's culture and context.
- Where possible, undergo basic training in trauma issues as an adjunct to core competency in case management.

WOMEN, PREGNANCY AND PARENTING

BARRIERS FACED BY WOMEN
The panel recommends that:
31. Case managers receive training and demonstrate awareness of the particular barriers to addiction treatment faced by women, including pregnant and parenting women. [III]

Women encounter unique barriers to treatment and face both social and internalized stigma. Gender-focused substance use treatment shows promising results (Hien & Levin, 1994; Zweben et al., 1994; Najavits et al., 2007; Stocco et al., 2002; Currie, 2001; Health Canada, 2006; Easton, 2006; Amodeo et al., 2004).

According to Health Canada (2001), some of the key issues in accessing substance use treatment that have a particular impact on women are:
- fear of losing children
- lack of affordable child care
- lack of family support
- social stigma
- lack of women-centred services
- cost of treatment
- lack of flexible services.

Understanding how gender-based differences affect treatment engagement, internalized stigma and treatment outcome will allow for a more responsive and sensitive approach to case management.

ISSUES FOR PARENTING CLIENTS

The panel recommends that:

32. Case managers act as information and referral agents for pregnant and parenting clients, and link these clients with services and resources that can help them access treatment, pre- and postnatal care and parenting support. [IV]

33. Case managers know and understand the legal and ethical issues involved in the requirement to inform child protection agencies of unstable or unsafe situations for parenting by MMT clients. [IV]

34. Case managers educate other agencies and the health care systems providing care to clients throughout pregnancy, during birth and post-natally about MMT. Case managers advocate on the clients' behalf so that the care they receive is based on informed decisions. [IV]

35. Case managers be aware of the special need for, and apply, an empathic, understanding and non-judgmental approach to interventions with pregnant or parenting clients, to maintain client engagement with treatment. [III]

Methadone maintenance treatment is the treatment of choice for opioid-dependent women who are pregnant. Opioid-dependent women who begin MMT during their pregnancy or who become pregnant while on MMT and their infants have better outcomes than opioid-dependent women not on MMT, including:

- an increased chance of avoiding miscarriage due to opioid withdrawal
- greater likelihood of their babies being born at full term and at higher birth weight than women who have untreated opioid dependency during pregnancy
- better engagement with prenatal health care services
- fewer health problems related to pregnancy.

Babies born to mothers on MMT may have symptoms of opioid withdrawal (neonatal abstinence syndrome), but these can and should be medically managed, so that babies born to opioid-dependent women on MMT generally have better outcomes than those babies born to women not being treated with methadone in an opioid-dependent pregnancy. Case management and outreach services increase treatment retention and involvement in prenatal medical care, and reduce substance use (Laken & Ager, 1996; CAMH, 2007; CPSO, 2005; Health Canada, 2001).

NEONATAL ABSTINENCE SYNDROME (NAS)

Neonatal abstinence syndrome occurs in most babies born to opioid-dependent mothers, including those on methadone. Infants with this syndrome are born with a dependence on opioids; they go into withdrawal after birth since they are no longer receiving opioids via the mother's bloodstream. They require the care of a neonatologist as they go through withdrawal.

PRACTICE POINT

CASE MANAGEMENT FOR PARENTS OF INFANTS WITH NAS

- Encourage the parents to have a thorough discussion with the doctor about what the syndrome is, what the symptoms are and what they need to do if they are concerned about the baby once they take it home from the hospital.
- Ensure that parents have an opportunity to discuss any questions they have about how to care for their newborn. Facilitate discussion between medical staff and the client, to review that under no circumstances should parents give the baby methadone or any other opioid, or any medication or substance not expressly approved by the doctor, even if the parents believe it will ease what they believe to be withdrawal symptoms, such as prolonged crying, disrupted sleep patterns or tremors.
- Encourage medical staff to have a clear discussion with new parents about what they will need to tell medical providers concerning the pregnancy and being on methadone in the event that they need to take their baby for urgent medical care. This includes honesty about any medication or opioids, including methadone, that the parents may have given their newborn. Failure to disclose this information will delay diagnosis and emergency medical care and could endanger the life of the infant.

PRACTICE POINT

COMMUNICATING WITH CLIENTS ABOUT HEALTH ISSUES

- Be very careful that you do not provide comments that could be misconstrued as "medical" advice or diagnostic interpretations in your discussion with clients about health issues. Be aware in your communication that there is room for error or misunderstanding on your part or on theirs.
- Be clear with clients about your role. Communicate with your clients that a chat with you is not a substitute for discussion with medical professionals and urge them to take their issues and questions to the appropriate care providers.

Case management can provide practical supports to pregnant women, such as assistance in finding stable housing, access to food and nutrition programs and referrals to parenting classes and supports.

While it is not routine for child protection services to become involved with pregnant clients on MMT, it is very likely that there will be some questions as to how stable the mother is in terms of drug use, housing and psychosocial supports as she nears delivery date. Care providers and hospital discharge planners may also have questions about the mother's significant others and/or the child's father in terms of their stability, drug use and relationship with the mother. Some hospitals, child protection agency workers and maternal care providers are familiar with MMT and may support the woman. Others may be misinformed about MMT and may stigmatize the woman, becoming overly scrutinizing and punitive, which may lead to unwarranted decisions about the client's ability to parent.

Case managers can serve as advocates for the woman and child, and as co-ordinators for the services and agencies that may be involved in the care of an MMT client who gives birth and of the infant.

In situations where children are being parented by a client with ongoing substance use and there are indicators of instability and risk to the safety and well-being of the children, a case manager has a legal duty to inform child protection services about these concerns. He or she should work with the client and the agency to formulate a treatment plan that is both supportive of the client and her evolving needs and in the best interests of her children.

GINA

SCENARIO: Gina is a 21-year-old opioid-dependent client who is seven months' pregnant. Gina has been using oral and injection opioids with her boyfriend since the age of 18. She has known about her pregnancy since she was five months' pregnant but only recently agreed to go on methadone. Gina's boyfriend, the father of her child, also enrolled in the program.

Gina is not sure if she wants to parent the child herself or give it up for adoption. She says that she still uses opioids but has cut back. She tells her case manager that her boyfriend still uses quite regularly and that this is a big trigger for her.

Gina and her boyfriend argue frequently, and Gina is not sure how long the relationship will last. She is anxious and concerned about her baby's health, and worried that being on methadone will harm the baby. Gina is also worried about having her baby taken away. She had a friend whose baby was taken away by the Children's Aid Society and she says that "for sure, they are going to think I'm a junkie and take my baby, too."

REFLECTION: The case manager understands that MMT is the optimal treatment for pregnant opioid-dependent clients and that keeping Gina engaged in treatment will raise the odds that she will improve her health and that of her unborn child. She understands that Gina may be involved with child protection services once her child is born and that Gina is understandably anxious about this situation. The case manager also acknowledges that Gina is ambivalent about her relationship with her boyfriend and about the idea of keeping her baby.

Continued on page 117

Continued from page 116

RESPONSE: The case manager provides Gina with information on pregnancy and methadone. She also arranges for Gina to have extra financial support so that she can eat more nutritiously. Gina receives prenatal care at a community health clinic familiar with methadone treatment. The case manager sometimes accompanies Gina to these appointments and then reviews and discusses with her the suggestions Gina receives from the nurse who is following her care, such as quitting smoking, eating well and refraining from alcohol and other drugs.

With Gina's agreement, the case manager invites Gina's boyfriend to attend some sessions, and discusses housing and support plans for the pair if they decide to stay together and parent their child. The case manager also talks with the couple about what will happen at the hospital. She arranges for them to meet the Children's Aid worker prior to the birth to answer questions and talk about what the worker will most likely be monitoring: stable housing, no drug use, attendance at parenting classes, continuing in substance use treatment and so on.

The case manager also takes time to ensure that both the Children's Aid worker and the hospital where Gina will give birth are aware of methadone treatment protocols and stigma issues, and asks to participate in forming Gina's discharge plan and to be included in any follow-up communications. The case manager checks in with Gina frequently about what kinds of supports she thinks might be helpful and how she is coping with the ambivalent feelings about her pregnancy and her boyfriend.

CLIENT CONSULTATION FINDINGS

PARENTING ISSUES

Over 40% of the clients surveyed stated that they had sought or would like assistance from a case manager for issues related to parenting and/or to child protection services.

CLIENTS TALK ABOUT
PREGNANCY AND PARENTING

"I have to take my toddler and my baby with me every day. Sometimes I would be one minute late getting off the bus with my kids and be too late with my urine screening. They didn't take this into consideration even though I asked them to. If I missed them before they closed for lunch I would have to wait over an hour with my kids outside or at the doughnut shop. If I didn't have any money I couldn't take my kids into the doughnut shop and we would have to be outside in the bad weather."

"I was pregnant and got on methadone. I'm doing good."

"I got on this program so I could clean up and get my kids back. I've been clean and on methadone and so is my husband but we are still waiting. It's very frustrating. A case manager could probably help out more. There is not a lot of communication with my Children's Aid worker and it's very frustrating."

"I frequently travel back and forth between town A and town B where my kids are. Because methadone is packaged and sent up from town T to town A, transferring back and forth is very difficult. It makes it hard to arrange visits. I can't always plan to see my kids; I have to plan weeks in advance so this makes it difficult."

"We need more clinics closer to home. It interrupts my work and weekends with my kids and having to travel in bad weather. I don't like to drive with my kids in the car when it's bad out. I've gone without and I was really sick."

"I lived in town S, a one-hour plane ride away. I moved to this town so I could be on the treatment. My whole family moved with me: my husband and three daughters."

PRACTICE POINT

SERVICES FOR PREGNANT AND PARENTING CLIENTS

- Understand the stress and challenges clients face in accessing and complying with MMT while caring for young children. Co-ordinate services for pregnant and parenting clients, and advocate to improve how services adapt to and support the needs of parents.
- Work with any other agencies that a pregnant or parenting client becomes involved with to ensure that they are informed about MMT and substance use. Encourage positive engagement and mutual problem-solving.
- Be aware of the professional obligations to report suspected child endangerment issues. Discuss any concerns and plans related to these issues with the MMT team.

PRACTICE POINT

BREASTFEEDING AND MMT

- Encourage clients to have specific discussions with their health care providers about breastfeeding while on methadone.
- Be aware that issues such as infant weight gain, the mother's use of other substances while breastfeeding and any feeding problems the baby may have can significantly affect the health of the newborn. Postnatal medical monitoring and follow-up are the best ways to address these concerns and are beyond the role of the case manager.
- Do not provide medical advice or suggestions about what to do, however well intentioned. Support and encourage clients to talk with their health care providers about any concerns or questions.

VIOLENCE

The panel recommends that:

36. Case managers receive training in working with clients who have experienced or are at risk of violence and trauma, specifically training in assessment, safety plans, and available community and legal resources. [III]

The issues of violence against women, violence within intimate partner relationships and violence and trauma experienced by clients in other ways are complex and interrelated, and a detailed discussion of them is beyond the scope of this guide. However, in order to effectively work with clients, case managers must have a thorough understanding and appreciation of these issues; therefore, it is highly important that they be a core component of case manager training.

Safety and disclosure are key areas around which case managers can provide clients with supportive counselling and help in accessing resources, coping with ambivalence and internalized shame, and addressing how the experience of violence and trauma may have contributed to their use of substances.

VIOLENCE

- Social and systemic factors such as socioeconomic inequity, cultural constraints and rigid socially determined gender roles contribute to the continuance of violence.
- Violence against women, in general and within intimate partner relationships, is experienced by a high percentage of women, across all age, cultural and socioeconomic categories.
- 67% of people in substance abuse treatment report histories of childhood abuse and neglect.
- Legal and judicial systems are often non-supportive and difficult to navigate for victims/survivors of violence.
- Sex trade workers are at increased risk for violence, but often they are not supported by legal and judicial systems when they report offences against them.
- The connection between experiences of abuse and violence and the correlation of emergent trauma symptoms such as

anxiety, depression and substance use has been well researched. Specialized treatment for these issues remains limited in many communities and the integration of these issues into generalized substance use treatment is variable.

For more information on the subject of violence against women, see Statistics Canada (2006), Health Canada (2006), Poole and Greaves (2007), Harrison and Carver (2004) and CSAT (2000a).

A CLIENT TALKS ABOUT VIOLENCE

"I was pregnant when I had to move from my house because of domestic violence. I couldn't easily transfer my prescription to my new area, and I was afraid to go back to my usual pharmacy because of my ex-partner so I went without methadone for two weeks. It was really hard."

PRACTICE POINT

WORKING WITH CLIENTS AND VIOLENCE ISSUES

- Include questions and discussion about immediate or past violence and trauma in a client's initial assessment. Encourage clients to talk about relationship difficulties.
- Be aware that many clients are ambivalent about leaving an abusive relationship.
- Be aware of the signs of relationship violence.
- Provide educational material about violence and trauma, including childhood abuse, relationship violence and violence experienced by women.
- Provide information on the legal rights of people who experience violence and on how to make a safety plan.
- Provide information about resources in the community that can offer safety, advice and emergency housing.
- Help to co-ordinate continuing methadone care for any clients who need to make abrupt changes in living or travel arrangements as a result of violence in their lives.

- Understand that there appears to be a strong relationship between experiences of violence and later perpetration of abuse. When working with MMT clients who are also perpetrators of abuse, reflect on any internalized bias and transference issues you may have. Familiarize yourself with risk assessment frameworks and make connections with community resources that provide counselling to clients with anger management and other behavioural issues related to violence.

For more on the subject of working with perpetrators of violence, see CSAT (2000a), Harrison and Carver (2004) and, in particular, Godden (2004).

EQUITY AND DIVERSITY

The panel recommends that:

37. Agencies and individuals providing case management demonstrate inclusion and awareness of equity and diversity. [IV]

38. Research bodies undertake further study to identify equity and diversity issues and their impact upon best practice of case management in MMT as it applies to Ontario communities and treatment models. [IV]

No formal study has been found on the issue of providing culturally sensitive services to MMT clients in Ontario, so the direct impact of the provision of such services on MMT outcomes in the province is not clear (Health Canada, 2006).

However, research led by Alexander et al. (2008) and Kehoe et al. (2003) found that attention to diversity issues in substance use counselling is an important part of providing culturally sensitive services and improving retention and outcomes.

Case managers can help to improve treatment engagement and outcomes if they incorporate into their practice an awareness and exploration of both their own and their clients' culturally based assumptions and beliefs. It is also important that case managers understand each client's social support systems, and discuss with clients who are immigrants or refugees the impact their expectations or experiences as a newcomer may have had on their substance use (CSAT, 2005; Harrison & Carver, 2004). On the strength of this evidence, the panel recommends that case managers demonstrate inclusion and awareness of diversity as part of best practice.

A study by Wood et al. (2007) involving Aboriginal people using injection opioids in British Columbia concluded that this population took longer to engage in and initiate MMT, and had higher drop-out rates and higher rates of HIV infection, hepatitis C infection and other drug use–related harms than non-Aboriginal users of injection drugs. The authors stated that there seemed to be significant barriers to enrolment and that these were largely related to service and treatment approaches that were not culturally sensitive; they concluded that further engagement strategies for this population were needed. No similar study for Ontario's Aboriginal populations was identified during the advisory panel's research.

LBGT ISSUES

This guide touches briefly on the importance of inclusion, diversity and equity and includes lesbian, gay, bisexual and transgendered considerations under the category of diversity and equity for case management best practice.

Case managers and programs should be aware that there are substantial issues in terms of knowledge, inclusive practice, treatment approaches, bias, social marginalization and systemic oppression that have a significant impact on how LBGT clients experience substance use treatment. This extensive body of knowledge and practice is beyond the scope of this guide.

We have included specific mention of this issue here to emphasize that commitment to respectful practice involves knowledge of these issues on a much more detailed and reflective level than we can provide here.

SPECIAL POPULATIONS: SENIORS

Case managers should approach the case management of seniors in MMT as they would that of other clients in terms of access to case management, empathic and respectful client-centred approaches, and referral and support to community agencies and services. Additional skills and areas of knowledge that can enhance this work include:
- an understanding of the biopsychosocial issues relevant to the aging process and opioid dependency
- an understanding of issues related to chronic pain and disease, and of their implications for methadone treatment
- an understanding of the cognitive and physical deficits that are common in aging adults and the impact these deficits have on the delivery of methadone maintenance services
- strong advocacy and referral skills, to collaborate with other systems that the client may be involved in, such as nursing homes, long-term care facilities and community services geared toward seniors
- an appreciation and awareness of the stigma that methadone-maintained seniors may encounter in their contact with various health care and social service providers
- a commitment to ongoing learning and knowledge enhancement based on emergent research about seniors and substance use.

PRACTICE POINT

IDEAS FOR BARRIER-FREE AND EQUITABLE PRACTICES

Be aware of and seek training in culturally competent practice. Ensure that materials and policies are welcoming and inclusive.

Features of a culturally competent practice include:
- mobility access to facilities (wheelchair access, grab bars, sufficient seating in the waiting room)
- change tables for infants
- educational materials provided in different languages, as appropriate to the local community, and accessible to clients at a wide range of literacy levels

- access to culturally competent interpretation services, including communication services to assist with hearing impairment or visual impairment
- flexibility in scheduling appointments to avoid conflict with religious practices
- posters and artwork that depict inclusivity through non-stereotypical images of people representing different ages, sexual orientations and cultural and ethnic groups
- clear agreements and policies that ask clients and staff to refrain from negative sexist or racial remarks
- staffing that reflects the community served
- a clear harassment and discrimination policy and mechanisms for client feedback about concerns they may have about their experiences with services.

TAM

SCENARIO: Tam is a 27-year-old client who has been on MMT for the past year. Tam is a newcomer to Canada and recently began working and attending ESL classes. He is enrolled in an apprenticeship program but frequently misses classes. Tam is still struggling with reducing his use, and his urine drug screening results show frequent opioid-positive samples. Tam has been reluctant to engage with his doctor and case manager to discuss what is happening in his life and what kinds of supports would help him make changes. One day Tam brings his older sister (who is also his sponsor) with him when he meets with the case manager.

Tam's sister explains that she has been in Canada for the past 10 years, whereas Tam recently arrived from their country of origin. She tells the case manager that their parents and extended family no longer speak to Tam or acknowledge him because he uses drugs; in their culture, such activity is considered shameful and dishonourable. Back home, people who use drugs are often punished by harsh jail time or even executed. Tam's sister expresses support for Tam and tells the case manager she is

Continued on page 126

Continued from page 125

concerned that he does not seem to be improving "even though he has opportunities here in Canada for a better life."

Tam says he has thought about talking to a worker at the cultural centre where he has his English classes but that "in my culture, they hate drug users, and they will not understand me. I do not want to see a worker there."

REFLECTION: The case manager understands that a client's cultural background can affect how he or she views treatment. In particular, a client's level of trust in and willingness to disclose to someone in a perceived position of authority, coupled with cultural assumptions about drug use, can affect the way he or she engages with, or disengages from, treatment.

RESPONSE: The case manager thanks Tam and his sister for talking about these difficult matters. He reflects with Tam on how difficult it must be to undergo MMT without the support of his parents. Together, he and Tam explore the value of continuing with counselling and case management to provide support and encouragement so Tam can move toward his goals. The case manager respects Tam's request that he not seek assistance from a service provider from his own cultural group at this time.

The case manager encourages Tam to bring his sister to sessions if he likes, and he provides Tam's sister with information booklets about MMT.

CLIENT CONSULTATION FINDINGS

DIVERSITY

Nearly 80% of the clients interviewed ranked an understanding of and respect for culture, religion, sexual orientation or other issues of diversity as extremely important qualities they would like to see in someone who provides them with case management services.

Program structures

The panel recommends that:
39. The Local Health Integration Networks provide funding to agencies and service providers so that they can implement and incorporate case management best practices into program structures and direct client care. [IV]

SUPPORTING THERAPEUTIC RELATIONSHIPS AND CLIENT ENGAGEMENT

The panel recommends that:
40. Programs are structured and funded so that the workload of case managers allows frequent brief contacts with MMT clients, particularly in the early stages of treatment, to allow relationship building. [III]

Case management and counselling are more effective when clients are engaged in a positive therapeutic relationship with the provider. Helping to meet clients' needs as they identify them, interacting in respectful and non-stigmatizing ways and offering non-confrontational support have been identified as positive factors in building relationships. Generally, therapist effects and qualities are as important as, if not more important than, the treatment modality used in terms of their effect on treatment outcomes (Hunt & Rosenbaum, 1998; Lilly et al., 2000; Longwell et al., 1978; Dennis et al., 1992; Gossop, Stewart et al., 2006; Orlinsky et al., 2004; Martin et al., 2000; CSAT, 2005).

The characteristics of counsellors that are most significantly associated with positive treatment outcomes and high levels of therapeutic alliances are good interpersonal skills (Najavits & Weiss, 1994) and respectful, empathic concern (Nelson-Zlupko et al., 1996).

It can be difficult to measure the development of the therapeutic relationship because it is not a quantifiable task or activity. Nevertheless, relationship building is one of the cornerstones of effective case management, and its positive impact has been documented in the literature. Developing a therapeutic relationship takes time; it is helped by:

- brief, frequent contact
- focused interventions
- the availability of case managers
- a supportive, client-centred clinic or agency atmosphere.

PRACTICE POINT

BUILDING A THERAPEUTIC RELATIONSHIP

- Provide opportunities when clients can drop in to see you, and make it a point to be visible and friendly when clients are attending other appointments in the clinic. Frequent brief, casual contact with case management is valued by clients and has a direct relationship to future engagement.
- Make contact with case management a "normal" part of methadone and clinic culture, not something that needs to take place only in response to a problem or concern. Clients may perceive that the only time they should speak to a case manager or seek counselling is when things are going badly. Asking for help is still seen culturally and socially by many people as a sign of weakness, and clients may be reluctant to initiate requests for assistance if they do not have a prior relationship with you.

CLIENTS TALK ABOUT
ACCESS TO CASE MANAGERS

"Always there when I need them. Willing to give a hand. They care."

"[There should be] more counsellors, lower caseloads."

"One time I really needed something, but I couldn't see my worker for two to three weeks. Better access would be good."

"I like to drop in and use the services. It gives me a focal point for my day, even if it's just for a few minutes."

"Knowing she is available if I need her . . . makes me feel better, more confident and able to cope."

"Just knowing someone is there I feel more comfortable."

"More individual treatment. You feel like you are just a number."

"It's hard not having a male counsellor available—some things I want to talk about with a man."

"I keep getting switched over to different workers. I used to see one weekly but now not so much."

The panel recommends that:

41. Programs provide case managers with ongoing supervision and opportunities for reflective practice so that they can continue to develop their therapeutic relationship skills. [IV]

PRACTICE POINT

PROFESSIONAL DEVELOPMENT

Enhance your skills by seeking, or creating, opportunities to reflect on client interactions and counselling strategies and learn about what worked and what did not. Training and self-study can assist with learning strategies, techniques and theories about client communication and effective engagement, but the real challenge is putting this into practice in "everyday life." Many professional education programs, such as those for social work and nursing, as well as some social service agencies, incorporate supervision and debriefing components into work with clients. Supervision by professional peers with opportunities for feedback and information sharing can be a helpful strategy in the absence of formal supervision resources.

CLIENTS TALK ABOUT
IMPORTANT QUALITIES FOR CASE MANAGERS

"Having staff that can relate and communicate well. Some staff don't understand or take time to get to the feelings."

"I've overheard staff talking about other clients and laughing at them. It was very inappropriate."

"Counsellors should be able to understand and relate to people."

"Be friendly and willing to help. Positive feedback is very helpful."

"One-on-one individual contact really helps to build trust."

"My worker ended up leaving and I had to get to know somebody new. It's hard to get used to a new person."

"They stick with me through thick and thin, no matter how much I'm using. They don't give up on me."

PROGRAM ORIENTATION

The panel recommends that:

42. Methadone providers and programs be educated and aware of the benefits of harm reduction approaches and non-punitive contingency management. [IIb]

43. The Ontario Ministry of Health and Long-Term Care support and require the collection of data, similar to that collected in DATIS, on the different MMT service delivery models and program orientations provided by OHIP-funded providers, and evaluate their outcome measures, including retention and client satisfaction with services. [IV]

PRACTICE PERSPECTIVES

"It really depends on the doctors. Some are very harm reduction–oriented and they will hang on to a client no matter how unstable they are or how much they use. Others will start tapering them if they won't stop using or they miss too many appointments. I really have to scramble to find other spots for these people.
—*Case Manager, Agency A*

"We really try to give people lots of chances here, but if they keep using and become really unstable, we transfer them to another program."
—*Case Manager, Agency B*

PRACTICE POINT

CLIENT-CENTRED PRACTICE

- Provide a mechanism for client feedback, and hold periodic discussions on the impact of program structure on clients' perceptions of treatment.
- Recognize the challenge inherent in ensuring that services are client-centred yet still efficiently run. Evaluate current ways of providing services to ensure that policies and processes are not overly restrictive or rigid.

CLIENTS TALK ABOUT
PROGRAM POLICY

"Increase trust, less restrictive policies, more attention to helping clients feel comfortable."

"Prescriptions here are dependent on your seeing a counsellor. You can't get a drink until you see them. If your drink is usually at 9:00 a.m. and your appointment is at 1:00 p.m. then you have to wait five hours for a drink."

"Agencies should be warm and welcoming. They should provide a good environment. People should have good communication skills. Empathy is important."

LOCATION AND ACCESS TO SERVICES

The panel recommends that:
44. Programs incorporate evening and weekend hours, as well as crisis response services, into their delivery of MMT case management services by partnering with other agencies and resources that provide this service. [IV]

The location and ease of access to MMT services, as well as to primary medical, psychiatric and social services, can greatly affect clients' engagement levels and program retention rates. Full-service MMT clinics may be able to provide a wide range of services under one roof and to offer flexible hours; for office-based practice, strong links to case management and community services can ensure that clients are optimally served. Clients may be reluctant or unable to seek out services on their own; however, case management can play an important linkage and referral role (Drucker et al., 2007; Friedmann et al., 2000, 2006).

Case management service that is flexible (e.g., provides evening and weekend hours, crisis response support) and offers practical assistance with transportation costs is very much valued by MMT clients (Friedmann et al., 2006).

CLIENT CONSULTATION FINDINGS

TRANSPORTATION ISSUES

Over half of the clients interviewed said they had experienced significant problems related to transportation to receive their methadone, and had sought or would like assistance from a case manager for help with these issues. The problems cited included:
- costs of transportation
- type of transportation available
- travel time
- having to rely on others for transportation.

CLIENTS TALK ABOUT
ACCESS ISSUES

"Better hours on weekends would be helpful."

"They are very busy at the clinic so I understand that I have to wait, but sometimes it isn't possible because I have to be at work."

"Have more workers here. There is not enough time to help everyone. More people would attend for counselling because it would be easier to get to and more people would use it."

"Evening hours enable me to go to work and get the counselling I need."

"Have in-person and telephone sessions."

PRACTICE POINT

FLEXIBLE HOURS

If at all possible, offer flexible hours; they are highly valued by clients and are shown to improve retention and outcome, yet few programs in Ontario offer them. This problem can be challenging to address given that program resources are usually limited.

Some suggestions:
- Consider opening later and closing later one day of the week, for example, every Wednesday the clinic runs from 12 noon to 7:00 p.m. instead of 9:00 a.m. to 5:00 p.m.
- Consider extended hours during which people do not come to the clinic but can contact a worker by phone.
- Partner with agencies that offer round-the-clock service—such as distress lines, emergency outreach vans, street outreach services, crisis centres—and collaborate with them to be "back ups" for methadone clients in crisis.
- Many local hospitals have evening or after-hours on-call social work or mental health services. Investigate possible partnerships for urgent care for MMT clients.
- Ask your clients about their need for flexible and extended hours, and present the documented results to Local Health Integration Networks and other funding bodies as part of an advocacy strategy and funding request.
- In the meantime, help clients make a plan for situations that occur after hours or on weekends.

CLIENT CONSULTATION FINDINGS

ACCESS TO SERVICES

- Of the clients interviewed, 68% said that having more drop-in and crisis availability (e.g., weekend hours, telephone support, partnerships with 24-hour community crisis services) would substantially improve the delivery of case management and counselling services.
- Over 87% said that extended or flexible hours would substantially improve service.
- Three out of four clients felt that telephone support would substantially improve the way case management and services are delivered.

Other health and social services

ACCESS TO SERVICES

The panel recommends that:

45. Case managers, with the support of other treatment team members, advocate for improved access to urgent health-care and primary social services (such as shelter and financial support programs) for MMT clients. [III]

46. Case managers, with the support of the MMT team, act as referral agents to these service agencies and co-ordinate the delivery of their services. [III]

MMT clients often require a variety of services, programs and networks to meet their immediate and longer-term goals and needs. Some services are practical and immediate, such as medical care, food support programs, financial assistance, help with shelter and housing issues or child care. Others are have a longer time frame, such as employment programs or vocational training.

Making linkages and referrals for clients to the appropriate services is one of the prime functions of a case manager (Ridgely & Willenbring, 1992).

FOSTERING INCLUSIVITY

The panel recommends that:

47. All health and social service programs in Ontario be accessible to and inclusive of MMT clients. [IV]

48. The Ontario Ministry of Health and Long-Term Care and other funding bodies provide funding for awareness education and service mechanisms to social service programs, to assist them with making their services more inclusive of MMT clients. [IV]

There is no collection of Ontario data that identifies the health and social services that are open to MMT clients or those that are unable or reluctant to provide service to MMT clients. Anecdotal evidence from case managers and clients, however, suggests that people on MMT encounter barriers to services. Some services, for example, some residential addiction treatment centres and supportive housing recovery programs, state outright that they do not serve methadone clients; others have program structures and policies that make it very difficult for a client in MMT to succeed (for example, vocational programs that make travelling to a pharmacy to pick up or take medications difficult to schedule, and jails that do not facilitate co-ordinated discharge plans to ensure continuity of methadone dosing).

Case managers can provide advocacy on behalf of clients and work to educate these agencies, but making systemwide changes requires leadership from other sectors: program funders and regulators need to work to ensure that services do not remain exclusionary.

CLIENTS TALK ABOUT
OTHER SERVICES

"I needed to apply for assistance to cover the costs of driving."

"The extra help with housing and finances was very appreciated."

"[It's been helpful] getting referred to different programming and finding out what is available. I've always worked and now I'm on Ontario Works. I'm new to the system so it helps having a case manager to sort things through."

"[People need] help with lots of things: legal issues, applying for . . . tax credits, health issues—it helps to have someone sort it out."

"I need a family doctor, but there aren't any that are taking patients. Staff can't help me with this problem."

"[I need] help sorting out disability payments. Sometimes [the disability program] eliminates you from help because you are on methadone. I'm disabled due to a motor vehicle accident, but [the program] does not see it that way. The system needs to be fixed—case managers can help fix this."

CARLA

SCENARIO: Carla is a 53-year-old woman with a long history of opioid dependence. She used opium tea and paste, which were readily available in her country of origin, to manage hip and back pain and to cope with depression. She has not been able to reduce her use of illegal opioids since she arrived in Canada three years ago. She began MMT about six months ago after being seen by a doctor at an immigrant outreach health centre. Her English speaking skills are limited and she has multiple health problems.

Carla is a refugee, and she and her two teenage children have been living with friends. The conditions are very crowded and they have been asked to leave there in the next few weeks. Carla states that she is feeling very lonely and isolated, even though she is happy that her children have the chance to get a good education in this country. Carla works as a seamstress and often worries because she does not make enough money to pay rent and buy food for herself and her children.

REFLECTION: The case manager realizes that in addition to her MMT, Carla has multiple needs, many of them urgent: housing, primary medical care and financial support. He understands that addressing these needs will most likely result in improved outcomes for Carla. He acknowledges that navigating various social service systems can be confusing and difficult for someone in her position.

RESPONSE: The case manager arranges for translation and support services with a newcomer community agency. He helps Carla with completing forms and applications for financial support, talks with her about her working conditions and rights, and puts her in touch with a women's organization that provides support and advocacy to immigrant textile workers. The case manager also advocates for Carla to get regular medical care in addition to her methadone treatment, and provides her with information on community after-school programs for her children.

PRACTICE POINT

ACCESSING OTHER SERVICES

When working with clients who have multiple and urgent needs, be prepared to help them navigate housing, financial, employment and other service systems in the community if other supports to do this work aren't available. In resource-poor communities, the case manager may be the only person who can assist with these needs.

AN MMT-INCLUSIVITY CHECKLIST
FOR COMMUNITY SERVICES

- Does the program offer its services to clients on methadone?
- Do program staff and support staff have basic knowledge and training about MMT?
- Has this training included information about the pharmacology of methadone and prescribing and dispensing issues? The principles of harm reduction? Anti-stigma education?
- Have staff members had an opportunity to explore their attitudes and beliefs around methadone treatment?
- Do the staff members demonstrate comfort and skill in explaining MMT to other clients in the program who are not on MMT and who express negative reactions or attitudes about clients on methadone?
- Are written materials used in programming (such as 12-step-based workbooks or pamphlets) inclusive and respectful of clients on MMT?
- Are dosing arrangements made for methadone clients (pharmacy accessibility, onsite storage as necessary, etc.)? Are arrangements for urine drug screening in place for clients who are required to leave regular samples while in treatment?
- Is there ongoing contact and communication with a physician who can address methadone prescribing and dosage issues should they arise while the client is in treatment?

ALI

SCENARIO: Ali is a 45-year-old opioid-dependent client who has been on methadone for the past five years. Ali has made good progress with reducing his opioid use, and his urine drug screening results suggest that he has been completely abstinent from opioids for the past nine months. Ali continues to use cocaine once or twice per week, and says that he really wants to stop but has been unable to do so even though he has been regularly attending outpatient counselling. Cocaine is often readily available at his workplace (he is in the music industry), and most of his associates and co-workers use socially.

Ali feels that a residential treatment program would give him "a break from work from friends who use" and allow him to focus on stopping his cocaine use. He has contacted a residential treatment program in his community but was told that they could not take him because he is on methadone. Ali is very upset and asks his case manager for assistance.

REFLECTION: Ali's case manager realizes that many addiction treatment programs and other service agencies are reluctant to take on methadone clients. She understands that a lack of MMT supports (such as secure storage for take-home doses and dispensing arrangements with local pharmacies) and previous negative experiences with methadone clients are often contributing factors to this reluctance. She also knows that education and understanding about the nature of methadone treatment is not standardized among Ontario addiction treatment agencies and other health and community services.

RESPONSE: The case manager explains to Ali that some agencies are not prepared to take methadone clients into their residential settings, but that she hopes the situation will change. She works with Ali to find a residential treatment agency that will be able to accommodate his MMT. The case manager contacts the agency that refused to take Ali and offers to send in educational materials for staff and also to give a brief in-service talk about methadone treatment.

CLIENTS TALK ABOUT
BARRIERS TO OTHER SERVICES

"There is still a huge stigma about being on methadone. Counsellors should be aware of that. They should educate people."

"Counsellors in other services, like addiction and housing services, need to know more about methadone. Other services who have had a person on methadone who hasn't worked out blame the methadone rather than the person. So when I go to use the services, they have retarded ideas about me."

"Case managers have to advocate for us with other services."

"The halfway house won't let me have carries in the house. They say it isn't safe."

PRACTICE PERSPECTIVE

"We have had a few methadone clients at our [long-term supportive housing] program, but they never really worked out. They were on the nod a lot and the other clients got really upset because they felt those clients got to sit around stoned all day, and not get kicked out. Plus, we could never get hold of the doctors when we needed them, and sometimes the clients would have to miss house meetings because they had to go to the pharmacy. It just didn't work out."
—Program worker at Agency C, employed 10 years.

EMPLOYMENT

The panel recommends that:

49. Government programs and other bodies funding employment and vocational training programs identify and reduce barriers to their services for MMT clients. [III]

Employment is a key indicator of social adjustment and recovery in populations with problem substance use. MMT clients are often "slow responders" to structured employment programs and may need longer treatment times, more intensive case management and counselling support to succeed in vocational programs (Blankertz et al., 2004; Knealing et al., 2006; Lidz et al., 2004).

Studies from other countries suggest that many MMT clients faced social and systemic barriers to employment before they developed substance use problems, and continue to face them after they have stopped using (Dennis et al., 1993; Metzger & Platt, 1989). These barriers include:
- limited education
- poverty and its attendant discrimination
- residence in areas where well-paying jobs (well enough to support a family) are scarce
- criminal records (which make it difficult to gain an employer's trust).

People who live with these barriers often become profoundly discouraged over time. Many investigators recommend that vocational programs and case management services acknowledge and seek to address these systemic and internalized barriers (Lidz et al., 2004; SSAM, 2007; CSAT, 2000b).

No current comprehensive Canadian studies were found regarding MMT clients and employment, but it is reasonable to extrapolate that issues and concerns are similar.

STEVE

SCENARIO: Steve is a 25-year-old oral opioid user who has been on methadone for two years. He is doing well on methadone and has four take-home doses a week. Steve wants to get further training in construction and has recently enrolled in a work training program. He is finding it difficult to get to his job site early in the morning because the pharmacies in his town do not open before 8:00 a.m. He expresses frustration at this situation: "I really want to get to work, give something back, be a taxpayer just like everyone else, but I'm getting in trouble because I'm always late the days I have supervised doses, and the training program said I might lose my placement."

REFLECTION: The case manager understands that gainful employment is an indicator of social stability and a positive contributor to treatment outcome. He acknowledges that MMT clients often face logistical barriers to participation in employment that can impede full participation and hamper client motivation.

The case manager understands that employers' and vocational or educational programs' understanding and willingness to accommodate the needs of MMT clients vary and that clients may benefit from support and advocacy services in this area.

RESPONSE: The case manager offers to contact Steve's training supervisor, with Steve's permission, and explain the situation. He also suggests speaking with Steve's doctor about the situation and getting a letter of support requesting accommodation for Steve to go to his pharmacy on the days he needs to. The case manager explains to Steve that attending at the pharmacy and being enrolled in MMT qualifies as medical treatment and that employers and schools must make reasonable accommodations for people to attend to their medical needs. The case manager offers to put Steve in touch with a local legal service that can provide him with more information about his rights as a worker.

CLIENTS TALK ABOUT
WORK-RELATED ISSUES

"The pharmacy is open later. I can come after work now. It's made a big difference."

"I've lost jobs because a pharmacy wasn't close by and I took too much time off work to get my dose."

"It limits your ability to work if you can't [get your methadone] early in the morning. Ideally, 6:00 a.m. would be a good schedule. They open at 9:00 a.m."

"Frequent urine screens make it hard to work and have a life."

"Sometimes there is a problem with a prescription not being ordered and not followed up with where I drink, and the dose has been cancelled. When there is a problem, the clinic [where my doctor is] is closed. I drink after work so if there is a problem I have to go sick and miss my dose. Then I miss a day of work."

PRACTICE POINT

WORKING

Be aware of systemic barriers to employment and training programs for MMT clients. Be prepared to advocate and problem-solve.

INSTITUTIONAL BARRIERS

The panel recommends that:

50. Hospitals and correctional institutions function with an awareness of the direct impact that the continuity and consistency of methadone dosing has on clients within their systems. They ensure that their admission and discharge planning procedures allow clients timely access to their daily methadone dose. These institutions implement and standardize collaboration and communication processes with case managers so that clients receive seamless care and consistent dosing. [IV]

CLIENTS TALK ABOUT
METHADONE AND JAIL

"People should get their methadone in jail. . . . If you have any positive opioids in your urine drug screen you don't get your dose for two or three days."

"Case management should be available for people on methadone. We need better planning to get methadone when being released from jail. I have been without methadone for three days. I was released with no help or arrangements on the outside to get my methadone. It sets people up to commit crimes on the street. The guards laugh at me and say, 'You'll be back.' And you know what, they are right."

"You can miss your drink for a few days when you're discharged from jail. It's not organized well. You don't get your drink the day you are released. If you go to court that day, you go without your drink. It's messed up. It's the jail's problem."

PRACTICE POINT

JAIL

- Realize that the challenges affecting methadone dosing for clients moving in or out of the correctional system require systemic and institutional change. Advocacy is an important function of case management and the obstacles in the correctional system to MMT for clients present an excellent opportunity to put advocacy into action.
- Talk with the local institutions in your area before there is a crisis or an urgent issue. Explain the methadone dosing issue and ask how you can assist with this issue should the need arise.
- Facilitate communication with jails about discharge plans and continuance of methadone. Monitor and discuss concerns about jail admission and discharge with the MMT team. Advocate for changes to current systems that produce gaps in the continuance of methadone prescriptions.
- Talk with clients about how they might handle a situation where they are suddenly incarcerated. Discuss harm reduction strategies and safety issues, in particular the risks of overdose if they are without their methadone for a few days and decide to use illegal opioids.
- Discuss with clients the importance of clear communication with jail staff, and how to make a request for medical and social service, prisoner advocacy services or chaplaincy assistance to help with methadone co-ordination if needed.
- Encourage clients to make their needs known to jail staff in a non-escalated and helpful way, and to also contact their case management support networks in the community if at all possible.

DRUG USE AND HARM REDUCTION IN ONTARIO PRISONS

Research suggests that HIV and hepatitis-C transmission is an issue of concern in prisons. The availability of illegal and contra-band substances within Ontario prisons is reported by clients anecdotally, although not acknowledged by institutions themselves.

Although research about harm reduction demonstrates that the availability of clean injection and inhalation equipment, condoms, and education about safer use and safer sex make an important contribution to the reduction of transmissible diseases, these resources are not consistently available in prisons in Ontario.

Case managers need to be aware that clients who are incarcerated and choose to use substances will often not have access to resources that can reduce the harms of drug use. Open and frank dialogue with clients about these realities and continued advocacy for institutions to be more responsive to the need to reduce disease transmission are important strategies for case managers to consider.

The panel recommends that:

51. The Ontario Ministry of Health and Long-Term Care and the province's Local Health Integration Networks fund research to evaluate, or require funded agencies to evaluate, the systemic barriers to accessing health and social services for MMT clients in Ontario, and use this data to improve these services. [IV]

THE NEED FOR SYSTEMIC CHANGE

Case management in MMT requires concrete knowledge that can be applied to working directly with clients. However, the systems and structures within which the work is carried out are frequently challenging and fragmented. As discussed in Ridgley et al. (1992), ". . . this has been the frustration of many [front-]line workers—that they are assigned to the impossible task of making organizations behave differently toward their clients or making and implementing rational care plans within irrational systems of care."

Gaining perspective about the need for systemic change can help inform the practical, everyday challenges in the work that case managers do, and is a fundamental step in initiating positive change.

Technology and telemedicine

The panel recommends that:

52. The Ontario Ministry of Health and Long-Term Care ensure that evaluation and outcome measures associated with the use of technology, particularly telemedicine, including levels of client satisfaction, be available and used by these service programs delivering MMT case management services. [IV]

Computerized therapies, similar to those being used to aid with smoking cessation and to treat anxiety and depression, show promising results in improving efficacy of MMT. In a randomized control trial, Bickel et al. (2008) found that computerized behavioural therapy for opioid-dependent outpatients was helpful in delivering more comprehensive treatment in a context where service providers were otherwise restricted by the challenges of time and resource constraints. The authors caution that more research is needed into the cost-effectiveness of these services, however.

This method of delivering therapy may be a way to provide more comprehensive MMT services to remote communities in Ontario. A Health Canada best practices guide on providing outreach to women with substance use problems (Health Canada, 2006) states that Internet technology may improve accessibility of supports and counselling for clients living in remote or rural areas. Other studies and reports suggest that telemedicine can act as an important adjunct in the delivery of medical and mental health services (O'Reilly et al., 2007; Telemental Health and Teleaddictions Partnership, 2006; Keresztes & Shaw, 2002; Buist et al., 2000; Hogenbirk et al., 2006).

Our panel found no studies that review the use of telemedicine and other remote technologies for MMT-specific services in Ontario. Anecdotal evidence from clients and case managers on this issue is mixed. Many clients report that the convenience and increased access resulting from the use of these services are helpful, but many clients report that they find the technology impersonal, alienating and inhibiting, particularly when used to deliver counselling and case management services, and that these services do not encourage engagement with methadone treatment.

CLIENTS TALK
ABOUT TELEMEDICINE

"It's hard to sit here and talk, and if you feel like crying it's hard to cry to a computer screen. I just don't get to say what I want to say."

"Video contact can be difficult—the person just isn't there. It isn't the same. They can't see any emotion. You feel ridiculous just talking to a monitor. That is why I prefer a few other agencies. Someone is actually there."

"More one on one, no video. We should be able to talk to someone in person. Some [clients] don't care, they just want to get in and out, but I do. I need to talk."

"Set up video counselling via home computer; this would make life easier, and I would use it more."

"I have never seen the doctor or the counsellor in person since I started eight months ago. It feels impersonal. The actual time they speak and the way they do it doesn't justify the payments from OHIP. No other doctor would get a payment for this. How easy is that? Two to three minutes on a screen and not caring to visit us in eight months. There is no other specialist that would work like that."

PRACTICE POINT

TELEMEDICINE

- Seek out training and supervision for supporting clients effectively in telemedicine formats, keeping in mind the lack of research about methadone treatment and the use of telemedicine in the delivery of counselling and case management services.
- Talk with clients about how they view telemedicine services. Explore with them what might put them at ease and what their concerns are, and offer to accompany clients to their telemedicine appointments. Communicate any concerns they or you have about telemedicine to the MMT team.

SECTION III: BEYOND THE RECOMMENDATIONS

Research gaps

In the course of developing this guide, the Working Advisory Panel identified a number of significant gaps in the existing research on case management and MMT.

In particular, the panel suggests that the following areas be considered for further research:

- the impact of standardized training of case managers on treatment retention and outcomes
- the impact of culturally appropriate outreach, case management and program structures on treatment retention and outcomes
- the efficacy of current Ontario program delivery systems and their impact on treatment retention and outcome
- the current barriers to service for northern, rural and isolated populations, and how these barriers might be reduced or eliminated
- the needs of Ontario health and social service providers in order to become more inclusive of and accessible to clients on MMT
- the ways that technology and telemedicine are being used in the delivery of MMT case management services and the impact they have on treatment retention and outcomes
- the impact that supervision of urine drug screens by persons acting in a case management function has on treatment retention and outcomes
- the impact of high caseloads and insufficient case management resources on treatment retention and outcomes.

Many of the recommendations of this guide are based on expert opinion and consensus and descriptive studies (levels III and IV). Further research is needed to validate and confirm the recommendations. More generally, the panel found the lack of Ontario-specific research to be a concern. Much of the existing research on case management is international in origin.

Case management is very much affected by social and environmental context. Criminal justice systems, housing and financial supports, access to health care and other support systems vary greatly from country to country and affect how clients experience substance dependence and treatment programs. These different conditions also influence the scope and role of case managers. What works in case management in the United Kingdom or the United States or Switzerland may not be applicable to Canada except in very broad terms; even within Canada, the circumstances under which case management is practised from province to province vary to the extent that study results are not easily extrapolated to case management in Ontario. Within the province, conditions and resources for case management and other services vary, and there are often marked differences between rural and urban service delivery systems.

Expanding and improving the level and quality of research will better inform the practice of case management and the delivery of MMT services.

In addition, as discussed under the heading "The Working Advisory Panel" in Section I, the panel hopes that future panels revising this guide will have the opportunity to include representatives from agencies not funded by the Ministry of Health and Long-Term Care, so as to provide a more complete picture of the case management settings, treatment and case management services offered in the province.

Implementation strategies

Finding support for change and implementing change into existing service delivery is a challenging process. Agencies that wish to incorporate the best practice recommendations for case management into their service delivery systems may consider the following strategies:

- **Appoint a "champion."** This person will be responsible for providing leadership and support to the guideline implementation. Ideally, the champion should have clinical skills and a thorough understanding of the components of MMT. Smaller agencies and group medical practices might want to consider pooling resources or collaborating with outside agencies and services to reduce the resource demands of the implementation process.
- **Perform an organizational gap analysis.** This assessment will help to identify how the program's current operating system fits with the recommendations and where the gaps are.
- **Establish a steering committee.** This committee, composed of key stakeholders and interdisciplinary team members, will be charged with overseeing the steps and strategies needed to align current practice with the guide's recommendations.
- **Revise program design and service delivery as necessary.** This process should include clear definitions about the target population, goals and objectives, outcome measures, required resources and evaluation activities.
- **Provide educational sessions for staff.** These sessions should include specific training in the competencies and knowledge areas identified in the guide. CAMH provides accredited methadone-related training, including the Opiate Dependence Treatment Interprofessional Education Program, and could be involved as a consultant on an in-house or external training provision. Education should be tailored to the specific environments of the agency (for example, the needs of a family service team will be different from those of a stand-alone methadone clinic).

- **Enlist organizational support.** Employers should provide their staff with the time and other resources they need to attend training sessions and to participate in implementation and evaluation activities on a regular basis.
- **Take a team approach.** Multidisciplinary participation makes for a more effective implementation team, as does involving clients and family members.
- **Connect with other support services.** Holistic MMT case management care involves collaboration with many different service agencies. MMT case management agencies should encourage these services to receive training about MMT and about how to implement best practice in working with MMT clients.
- **Take a system approach.** Within addiction and mental health system networks, review the provision of case management for MMT clients and recommend to Local Health Integration Networks the appropriate model of service, the number of case management providers, the suggested providers and the linkages within the system.

Smaller agencies, and loosely structured service delivery systems in particular, may lack the resources to facilitate the implementation of change. Agencies are encouraged to present their implementation strategies and learning needs to their Local Health Integration Networks as one possible way to secure funding for implementing best practices. The Working Advisory Panel also encourages Ontario's Ministry of Health and Long-Term Care to take on a leadership role in providing financial support to agencies and service providers for incorporating best practice recommendations into their program structures and client care.

Evaluation and monitoring

Another important aspect of the adoption of best practice guidelines is monitoring their implementation and assessing the impact on outcomes.

Table 6, adapted from a framework developed by the Best Practice Guide program of the Registered Nurses' Association of Ontario (RNAO, 2002), gives some examples of how this might be done for various levels and categories of stakeholders (system, organization, individual manager or MMT team, client) and from the point of view of funding.

TABLE 6
Monitoring and evaluating the impact of implementing best practice guidelines: Some sample measures

SYSTEM

Structure	• Interorganizational structures (LHIN committees, interagency meetings, intersectoral meetings) identify key providers within the system and enable the implementation and co-ordination of recommended practices.
Process	• Regular communication and co-ordination occurs among stakeholder groups. • Stakeholders (community pharmacists, family health teams, methadone clinics, LHINS, clients, addiction agencies, hospitals, corrections) share data, identify service gaps, communicate and problem-solve together.
Outcome	• Improved access enables co-ordinated, comprehensive, community-based MMT for people with opioid addiction.

- Fewer incidents of overdose, opioid-addiction-related crime, opioid-addiction-related suicide, etc.
- MMT incorporates case management services matched to clients' needs regardless of their geographic location.
- A rise in the percentage of programs in a given area that have a physician and pharmacist trained to support best practice in case management.

ORGANIZATION

Structure
- The organization has a best practice review committee.
- Sufficient funds provide case managers with ongoing professional development, including education about best practices.
- The organization supports knowledge sharing within teams, identifies champions and provides mentorship opportunities to new staff.

Process
- The committee acts on best practice recommendations and makes changes to current policies and procedures consistent with the recommendations of the best practice guide.

Outcome
- The organization's policies and procedures related to MMT are consistent with best practice recommendations.
- Structured documentation in clients' heath records reflects assessment and case management services that are consistent with best practice.
- The organization's MMT providers have access to a case manager trained in best practice.
- The programs delivered by the organization have access to physicians and pharmacists trained to support best practices in case management.
- The organization assesses increases in treatment retention, reductions in high-risk behaviour and increases in social stability and function.

CASE MANAGER/MMT TEAM

Structure   • The MMT team has at least one case manager
trained in best practice whose role is to mentor
others.

Process   • Case managers attend and complete educational
sessions regarding best practice in MMT case
management (such as the CAMH Opiate Dependence
Treatment certificate program, Canadian Society
of Addiction Medicine conferences and CPSO
conferences).
   • Case managers and other MMT team members
self-assess their
   – knowledge of assessment and treatment matching,
engagement and retention strategies, harm reduction
and health education
   – liaison and advocacy skills (in order to ensure
access to needed support services)
   – understanding of stigma and bias issues
   – knowledge of counselling approaches
   – knowledge of mental health, trauma, diversity,
gender, marginalization and treatment issues
affected by the above.

Outcome   • Case managers and other MMT team members
display increased knowledge about how to support
best practice in case management.
   • Documentation in clients' health records by physicians
and pharmacists reflects the integration of best
practices for case management.

CLIENT

Structure   • Clients are involved in interorganizational (systemwide) MMT committees.

Process   • Client input has resulted in changes to processes.

Outcome   • Clients' satisfaction with services has improved;
they feel respected and have better health. They
remain in treatment and do not drop out prematurely.
Participation in treatment becomes less disruptive
to their daily lives. Barriers to work, school and
health and community services are reduced.

FINANCIAL COSTS

Structure	• Adequate financial and human resources provide for guideline implementation. • An appropriate budget funds education, adequate staffing and on-the-job supports. • New assessment, documentation and data collection systems are in place.
Process	• Resources are applied to best practice implementation and its impact is monitored.
Outcome	• Return on investment for case management delivery to MMT clients has improved.

Process for updating and review

CAMH proposes to update this best practice guide as follows:
- The guide will be reviewed by a team of case management and methadone specialists every three years.
- During the three-year period between development and revision, the CAMH Methadone Maintenance Treatment Education Executive Committee will regularly monitor for new systematic reviews, randomized controlled trials and other relevant literature in the field.
- Based on the results of this monitoring, the Committee may recommend an earlier revision period. Appropriate consultation with a team comprising the original advisory panel members and other specialists in the field will help inform any decision to review and revise the guidelines earlier than the three-year milestone.
- Three months prior to the three-year review milestone, the Committee will commence planning of the review process by:
  - inviting specialists in the field to participate on the review team (the review team will comprise members from the original panel as well as other specialists; additionally, input and dialogue from the Ontario College of Social Work and Social Service Workers will be sought regarding updates in the certification and educational requirements for case manager training)
  - compiling feedback received and questions encountered during the dissemination of the current guide as well as any information gathered from the experiences of organizations implementing the recommendations
  - compiling any new clinical practice guidelines in the field, systematic reviews, meta-analysis papers, technical reviews, randomized controlled trial research and other relevant literature
  - developing a detailed work plan with target dates and deliverables.

The revised guideline will undergo dissemination based on established structures and processes.

References

Alexander, J., Nahra, T., Lemak, C., Pollack, H. & Campbell, C. (2008). Tailored treatment in the outpatient substance abuse treatment sector: 1995–2005. *Journal of Substance Abuse Treatment, 34* (3), 282–292.

Alterman, A. & Cacciola, J. (1991). The antisocial personality disorder in substance abusers: Problems and issues. *Journal of Nervous and Mental Disease, 179* (7), 401–409.

American Psychiatric Association (APA). (2006). *Practice Guideline for the Treatment of Patients with Substance Use Disorder* (2nd ed.). Arlington, VA: Author.

Amodeo, M., Chassler, D., Ferguson, F., Fitzgerald, T. & Lundgren, L. (2004). Use of mental health and substance abuse treatment services by female injection drug users. *American Journal of Drug and Alcohol Abuse, 30* (1), 101–120.

Australian Department of Health and Ageing, National Drug Strategy. (2003). *Principles of Drug Addiction Treatment: A Research-Based Guide.* Canberra, Australia: Author.

Ball, J. & Ross, A. (1991). *The Effectiveness of Methadone Maintenance Treatment.* New York: Springer.

Ball, S., Martino, S., Nich, C., Frankforter, T., Van Horn, D., Crits-Christoph, Z.P. et al. (2007). Site matters: Multisite randomized trial of motivational enhancement therapy in community drug abuse clinics. *Journal of Consulting and Clinical Psychology, 7* (4), 556–567.

Barry, D., Bernard, M., Beitel, M., Moore, B., Kerns, R. & Schottenfeld, R. (2008). Counselors' experiences treating methadone-maintained patients with chronic pain: A needs assessment study. *Journal of Addiction Medicine, 2* (2), 108–111.

Bell, J. (1998). Delivering effective methadone treatment. In J. Ward, R. Mattick & W. Hall (Eds.), *Methadone Maintenance Treatment and Other Opioid Replacement Therapies* (pp. 161–175). Amsterdam: Harwood Academic.

Bickel, W., Buchalter, A., Marsch, L. & Badger, G. (2008). Computerized behavior therapy for opioid-dependent outpatients: A randomized control trial. *Experimental and Clinical Psychopharmacology, 16* (2), 132–143.

Blankertz, L., Magura, S., Staines, G., Madison, E., Spinelli, M., Horowitz, E. et al. (2004). A new work placement model for unemployed methadone maintenance patients. *Substance Use and Misuse, 39* (13 & 14), 2239–2260.

Booth, R., Corsi, K. & Mikulich-Gilbertson, S. (2004). Factors associated with methadone maintenance treatment retention among street-recruited injection drug users. *Drug and Alcohol Dependence, 74,* 177–185.

British Columbia Ministry of Health (BC MOH). (2005). *Harm Reduction: A British Columbia Community Guide*. Victoria, BC: Author.

Brown, T. & Dongier, M. (2005). Availability and use of evidence-based treatment. In G. Roberts, G. Graves & J. Weekes (Eds.), *Substance Abuse in Canada: Current Challenges and Choices* (pp. 23–29). Ottawa: Canadian Centre on Substance Abuse.

Buist, A., Coman, G. & Silvas, A. (2000). An evaluation of the telepsychiatry programme in Victoria, Australia. *Journal of Telemedicine and Telecare, 6*, 216–221.

Center for Substance Abuse Treatment (CSAT). (2000a). *Substance Abuse Treatment for Persons with Child Abuse and Neglect Issues*. Treatment Improvement Protocol (TIP) series, no. 36. Rockville, MD: U.S. Substance Abuse and Mental Health Services Administration (SAMHSA).

Center for Substance Abuse Treatment (CSAT). (2000b). *Integrating Substance Abuse Treatment and Vocational Services*. Treatment Improvement Protocol (TIP) series, no. 38. Rockville, MD: U.S. Substance Abuse and Mental Health Services Administration (SAMHSA).

Center for Substance Abuse Treatment (CSAT). (2005). *Medication-Assisted Treatment for Opioid Addiction in Opioid Treatment Programs: Approaches to Providing Comprehensive Care and Maximizing Patient Retention*. Treatment Improvement Protocol (TIP) series, no. 43. Rockville, MD: U.S. Substance Abuse and Mental Health Services Administration (SAMHSA).

Centre for Addiction and Mental Health (CAMH). (2007). *Exposure to Psychotropic Medication and Other Substances During Pregnancy and Lactation: A Handbook for Health Care Providers*. Toronto: Author.

Centre for Addiction and Mental Health (CAMH). (2008). *Methadone Maintenance Treatment: Client Handbook*. Toronto: Author.

Chatham, L., Knight, K.G., Joe, G., Brown, B. & Simpson, D. (1995). Suicidality in a sample of methadone maintenance clients. *American Journal of Drug and Alcohol Abuse, 21* (3), 345–361.

Collège des médecins du Québec & Ordre des pharmaciens du Québec. (2000). *Clinical guidelines and procedures for the use of methadone in the maintenance treatment of opioid dependence*. Quebec City: Author.

College of Physicians and Surgeons of Ontario (CPSO). (2005). *Methadone Maintenance Guidelines*. Toronto: Author.

Connock, M., Juarez-Garcia, A., Jowette, S., Frew, E., Liu, Z., Taylor, R. et al. (2007). Methadone and buprenorphine for the management of opioid dependence: A systematic review and economic evaluation. *Health Technology Assessment, 11* (9), 1–171.

Copenhaver, M., Bruce, R. & Altice, F. (2007). Behavioral counseling content for optimizing the use of buprenorphine for treatment of opioid dependence in community based settings: A review of the empirical evidence. *American Journal of Drug and Alcohol Abuse, 33* (5), 643–654.

Courtwright, D., Herman J. & DesJarlais, D. (1989). *Addicts Who Survived: An Oral History of Narcotic Use in America, 1923–1965*. Knoxville, TN: University of Tennessee Press.

Csete, J. (2007). *Do Not Cross: Policing and HIV Risk Faced by People Who Use Drugs*. Toronto: Canadian HIV/AIDS Legal Network.

Currie, J. (2001). *Best Practices Treatment and Rehabilitation for Women with Substance Use Problems*. Report prepared for Canada's Drug Strategy, Health Canada. Ottawa: Health Canada.

Darke, S., Hall, W. & Swift, W. (1994). Prevalence, symptoms and correlates of antisocial personality disorder among methadone maintenance clients. *Drug and Alcohol Dependence, 34* (3), 253–257.

Darke, S. & Ross J. (2001). The relationship between suicide and heroin overdose among methadone maintenance patients in Sydney, Australia. *Addiction, 96* (10), 1443–1441.

Dennis, M., Karuntzos, G., McDougal, G., French, M. & Hubbard, R. (1993). Developing training and employment programs to meet the needs of methadone treatment clients. *Evaluation and Program Planning, 16* (2), 73–86.

Dennis, M., Karuntzos, G. & Rachal, J. (1992). Accessing additional community resources through case management to meet the needs of methadone clients. In R. Ashery (Ed.), *Progress and Issues in Case Management.* National Institute on Drug Abuse Research Monograph No. 127 (pp. 54–78). Washington, DC: NIDA.

DiClemente, C. & Velasquez, M. (2002). Motivational interviewing and the stages of change. In W. Miller & S. Rollnick (Eds.), *Motivational Interviewing: Preparing People for Change* (2nd ed.) (pp. 201–216). New York: Guilford.

Drucker, E., Rice, S., Ganse, G., Kegley, J., Bonuck, K. & Tuchman, E. (2007). The Lancaster office-based opiate treatment program: A case study and prototype for community physicians and pharmacists providing methadone maintenance treatment in the United States. *Addictive Disorders and Their Treatment, 6* (3), 121–136.

Dzialdowski, A., London, M. & Tillbury, J. (1998). A controlled comparison of cognitive behavioral and traditional counseling in a methadone tapering program. *Clinical Psychology and Psychotherapy, 5,* 47–53.

Easton, C. (2006). The role of substance abuse in intimate partner violence. *Psychiatric Times, 23* (special report, 1), 26–27.

Farrell, M., Neeleman, J., Gossop, M., Griffiths, P., Buning, E., Finch, E. et al. (1996). *A Review of the Legislation, Regulation and Delivery of Methadone in 12 Member States of the European Union.* Brussels, Belgium: The European Commission.

Fiellin, D., Pantalon, M., Chawarski, M., Moore, B., Sullivan, C., O'Connor, P. et al. (2006). Counseling plus buprenorphine: Nalaxone maintenance therapy for opioid dependence. *New England Journal of Medicine, 355,* 365–374.

Fischer, B., Capre, D., Daniel, N. & Gliksman, L. (2002). *Methadone Treatment in Ontario after the 1996 Regulation Reforms: Results of a Physician Survey.* Toronto: Centre for Addiction and Mental Health.

Fischer, B., Patra, J., Cruz, M., Gittins, J. & Rehm, J. (2008). Comparing heroin users and prescription opioid users in a Canadian multi-site population of illicit opioid users. *Drug and Alcohol Review,* Mar 31, 1–8.

Fischer, B., Rehm, J., Patra, J. & Firestone-Cruz, P. (2006). Changes in illicit opioid use across Canada. *Canadian Medical Association Journal, 175* (11), 1385–1387.

Friedmann, P., D'Aunno, T., Jin, L. & Alexander, J. (2000). Medical and psychosocial services in drug abuse treatment: Do stronger linkages promote client utilization? *Health Services Review, 35* (2), 443–465.

Friedmann, P., Hendrickson, J., Gerstein, D., Zhang, Z. & Stein, M. (2006). Do mechanisms that link addiction treatment patients to primary care influence subsequent utilization of emergency and hospital care? *Medical Care, 44* (1), 8–15.

Futterman, R., Lorente, M. & Silverman, S. (2005). Beyond harm reduction: A new model of substance abuse treatment further integrating psychological techniques. *Journal of Psychotherapy Integration, 15* (1), 3–18.

Giyaur, K., Sharf, J. & Hilsenroth, M. (2005). The Capacity for Dynamic Process Scale (CDPS) and patient engagement in opiate addiction treatment. *Journal of Nervous and Mental Disease, 193* (12), 833–838.

Godden, T. (2004). Working with men. In S. Harrison & V. Carver (Eds)., *Alcohol and Drug Problems: A Practical Guide for Counsellors* (pp. 273–297). Toronto: Centre for Addiction and Mental Health.

Goldstein, M., Deren, S., Kang, S., Des Jarlais, D. & Magura, S. (2002). Evaluation of an alternative program for MMTP drop outs: Impact on treatment re-entry. *Journal of Drug and Alcohol Dependence, 66,* 181–187.

Gossop, M., Marsden, J. & Stewart, D. (2006). Remission of psychiatric symptoms among drug misusers after drug dependence treatment. *Journal of Nervous and Mental Disease, 194* (11), 826–832.

Gossop, M., Stewart, D. & Marsden, J. (2003). Treatment process components and heroin use outcome among methadone patients. *Drug and Alcohol Dependence, 71,* 93–102.

Gossop, M., Stewart, D. & Marsden, J. (2006). Effectiveness of drug and alcohol counselling during methadone treatment: Content, frequency and duration of counselling and association with substance use outcomes. *Addiction, 101,* 404–412.

Gourevitch, M., Chatterji, P., Nandini, D., Schoenbaum, E. & Turner, B. (2007). On-site medical care in methadone maintenance: Associations with health care use and expenditures. *Journal of Substance Abuse Treatment, 32,* 143–151.

Harrison S. & Carver, V. (Eds.) (2004). *Alcohol and Drug Problems: A Practical Guide for Counsellors.* Toronto: Centre for Addiction and Mental Health.

Havens, J. & Strathdee, S. (2005). Antisocial personality disorder and opioid treatment outcomes: A review. *Addictive Disorders and Their Treatment, 4* (3), 85–98.

Hawkings, C. & Gilburt, H. (2004). *Dual Diagnosis Toolkit: Mental Health and Substance Use.* London, UK: Turning Point and Rethink (copublishers).

Health Canada. (1999). *Best Practices: Substance Abuse Treatment and Rehabilitation.* Ottawa: Minister of Public Works and Government Services.

Health Canada. (2001). *Best Practices: Treatment and Rehabilitation for Women with Substance Use Problems.* Ottawa: Minister of Public Works and Government Services.

Health Canada. (2002a). *Best Practices: Methadone Maintenance Treatment.* Ottawa: Minister of Public Works and Government Services.

Health Canada. (2002b). *Best Practices: Concurrent Mental Health and Substance Use Disorders.* Ottawa: Minister of Public Works and Government Services.

Health Canada. (2006). *Best Practices: Early Intervention, Outreach and Community Linkages for Women with Substance Use Problems.* Ottawa: Health Canada.

Hien, D. & Levin, F. (1994). Trauma and trauma-related disorders for women on methadone: Prevalence and treatment considerations. *Journal of Psychoactive Drugs, 26* (4), 421–429.

Hogenbirk, J., Montgomery, D., Boydell, K., Pong, R. & Cudney, D. (2006). *Using Telehealth to Augment Delivery of Mental Health Services by Family Health Teams: Potential Barriers and Possible Solutions.* Final report submitted to Ontario Ministry of Health and Long-Term Care and Ontario Mental Health Foundation. Sudbury, ON: Centre for Rural and Northern Health Research, Laurentian University.

Hunt, G. & Rosenbaum, M. (1998). "Hustling" within the clinic: Consumer perspectives on MMT. In J. Inciardi and L. Harrison (Eds.), *Heroin in the Age of Crack-Cocaine.* (pp. 188–214). Thousand Oaks, CA: Sage.

Joe, G., Simpson, D., Dansereau, D. & Rowan-Szal, G. (2001). Relationships between counseling rapport and drug abuse treatment outcomes. *Psychiatric Services, 52* (9), 1223–1229.

Johnson, S., van de Ven, J. & Grant, B. (2001). *Institutional MMT: Impact on Release Outcome and Institutional Behaviour.* Montague, PEI: Corrections Canada, Research Branch, Addictions Research Centre.

Kang, S., Magura, S., Nwakeze P. & Demsky, S. (1997). Counselor attitudes in methadone maintenance. *Journal of Maintenance in the Addictions, 1* (2), 41–58.

Kay, R. & Peters, A. (1992). A pilot survey of client opinion of the Lothian community drug problem service: Likes, dislikes, efficacy and improvements. *Health Bulletin* (Edinburgh), 50 (1), 32–38.

Kayman, D., Goldstein, M., Deren, S. & Rosenblum, A. (2006). Predicting treatment retention with a brief "Opinions about Methadone" scale. *Journal of Psychoactive Drugs, 38* (1), 93–100.

Kehoe, K., Melkus, G. & Newlin, K. (2003). Culture within the context of care: An integrative review. *Ethnicity and Disease, 13* (3), 344–353.

Keresztes, C. & Shaw, R. (2002). *Evaluation of the Keewaytinook Okimakanak Telepsychiatry Pilot Project.* Kingston, ON: Centre for Health Services and Policy Research, Queen's University.

Kidorf, M., Neufeld, K. & Broomer, R. (2004). Combining stepped care approaches with behavioral reinforcement to motivate employment in opioid dependent outpatients. *Substance Use and Misuse, 39* (13 & 14), 2215–2238.

Knealing, T., Wong, C., Diemer, K., Hampton, J. & Silverman, K. (2006). A randomized controlled trial of the therapeutic workplace for community methadone patients: A partial failure to engage. *Experimental and Clinical Psychopharmacology, 14* (3), 350–360.

Kosten, T. & Rounsaville, B. (1988). Suicidality among opiate addicts: 2.5 year follow-up. *American Journal of Drug and Alcohol Abuse, 14* (3), 357–369.

Krausz, M., Degwitz, P., Haasen, C. & Verthein, U. (1996). Opioid addiction and suicidality. *Crisis, 17* (4), 175–181.

Laken, M. & Ager, J. (1996). Effects of case management on retention in prenatal substance abuse treatment. *American Journal of Drug and Alcohol Abuse, 22* (3), 439–448.

Leshner, A.I. (1999). Science-based views of drug addiction and treatment. *Journal of the American Medical Association, 282* (14), 1314–1316.

Lidz, V., Sorrentino, D., Robison, L. & Bunce, S. (2004). Learning from disappointing outcomes: An evaluation of prevocational interventions for methadone maintenance patients. *Substance Use and Misuse, 39* (13 & 14), 2287–2308.

Lilly, R., Quirk, A., Rhodes, T. & Stimson, G. (1999). Juggling multiple roles: Staff and client perceptions of key worker roles and the constraints on developing counselling and support services in methadone treatment. *Addiction Research & Theory, 7* (4), 267–289.

Lilly, R., Quirk, A., Rhodes, T. & Stimson, G. (2000). Sociality in methadone treatment: Understanding methadone treatment and service delivery as a social process. *Drugs, Education, Prevention & Policy, 7* (2), 163–178.

Longwell, B., Miller, J. & Nichols, A.W. (1978). Counselor effectiveness in a MMT program. *International Journal of Addictions, 13* (2), 307–315.

Madden, A., Lea, T., Bath, N. & Winstock, A. (2008). Satisfaction guaranteed? What clients on methadone and buprenorphine think about their treatment. *Journal of Drug and Alcohol Review, 31,* 1–8.

Magura, S., Rosenblum, A., Fong, C., Villano, C. & Richman, B. (2002). Treating cocaine-using methadone patients: Predictors of outcomes in a psychosocial clinical trial. *Substance Use and Misuse, 37* (14), 1927–1955.

Martin, D., Garske, J. & Davis, M. (2000). Relation of the therapeutic alliance with outcome and other variables: A meta-analytic review. *Journal of Consulting and Clinical Psychology, 68,* 438–450.

Martin, G., Brands, B. & Marsh, D. (2003). *Methadone Maintenance: A Counsellor's Guide to Treatment.* Toronto: CAMH.

Mayet, S., Farrell, M., Ferri, M., Amato, L. & Davoli, M. (2008). Psychosocial treatment for opiate abuse and dependence. *The Cochrane Database of Systematic Reviews, volume 1.*

McCann, M.J., Rawson, R.A., Obert, J.L. & Hasson, A.L. (1994). *A Treatment of Opiate Addiction Using Methadone: A Counselor Manual.* Rockville, MD: Centre for Substance Abuse Treatment.

McLellan, A., Arndt, I., Metzger, D., Woody, G. & O'Brien, C. (1983). The effects of psychosocial services in substance abuse treatment. *Journal of the American Medical Association, 269,* 1953–1959.

McLellan, A., Weinstein R., Shen, Q., Kending, C. & Levine, M. (2005). Improving continuity of care in a public addiction treatment system with clinical case management. *American Journal of Addiction, 14* (5), 426–440.

Meichenbaum, D. & Turk, D. (1987). *Facilitating Treatment Adherence.* New York: Plenum.

Methadone Maintenance Treatment Practices Task Force. (2007). *Report.* Toronto: Ontario Ministry of Health and Long-Term Care.

Metzger, D. & Platt, J. (1989). Solving vocational problems for addicts in treatment. In J. Platt, C. Kaplan & P. McKim (Eds.), *The Effectiveness of Drug Abuse Treatment: Dutch and American Perspectives* (pp. 101–112). Malabar, FL: Krieger.

Montoya, I., Schroeder, J. & Preston, K. (2005). Influence of psychotherapy attendance on buprenorphine treatment outcome. *Journal of Substance Abuse Treatment, 28* (3), 247–254.

Najavits, L., Rosier, M., Nolan, A. & Freeman, M. (2007). A new gender-based model for women's recovery from substance abuse: Results of a pilot outcome study. *American Journal of Drug and Alcohol Abuse, 33,* 5–11.

Najavits, L. & Weiss, R, (1994). Variations in therapist effectiveness in the treatment of patients with substance use disorders: An empirical review. *Addiction, 89,* 679–688.

National Institute on Drug Abuse (NIDA), National Institute of Health. (1999a). *Drug Misuse and Dependence: Guidelines on Clinical Management.* Bethesda, MD: Author.

National Institute on Drug Abuse (NIDA), National Institute of Health. (1999b). *Principles of Drug Addiction Treatment: A Research-Based Guide.* Bethesda, MD: Author.

Nelson-Zlupko, L., Dore, M., Kauffman, E. & Kaltenbach, K. (1996). Women in recovery: Their perceptions of treatment effectiveness. *Journal of Substance Abuse Treatment, 13* (1), 51–59.

Newfoundland & Labrador Pharmacy Board. (2007). *Standards of Pharmacy Practice for the Newfoundland and Labrador Methadone Maintenance Program.* St. John's, NL: Author.

New South Wales Opioid Treatment Program. (2006). *Clinical Guidelines for Methadone and Buprenorphine Treatment of Opioid Dependence.* New South Wales, Australia: Mental Health and Drug and Alcohol Office, Department of Health.

Ontario Addiction Services Advisory Council. (2000). *Admission and Discharge Criteria for Ontario's Substance Abuse Services.* Toronto: Ontario Substance Abuse Bureau, Ministry of Health and Long-Term Care.

Ontario Ministry of Health and Long-Term Care. (2008). *Interprofessional Care: A Blueprint for Action in Ontario.* Submitted by the Interprofessional Care Steering Committee. Toronto: Author.

O'Reilly, R., Bishop, J., Maddox, K., Hutchinson, L., Fisman, M. & Takhar, J. (2007). Is telepsychiatry equivalent to face to face psychiatry? Results from a randomized controlled equivalence trial. *Psychiatric Services, 58* (6), 836–843.

Orlinsky, D., Roonnestad, M. & Wilutzki, U. (2004). Fifty years of psychotherapy process-outcome research: Continuity and change. In M.J. Lambert (Ed.), *Bergin and Garfield's Handbook of Psychotherapy and Behavior Change* (5th ed.). New York: John Wiley & Sons.

Phillips, K. & Rosenberg, H. (2008). The development and evaluation of the Harm Reduction Self-Efficacy Questionnaire. *Psychology of Addictive Behaviors, 22* (1), 36–46.

Platt, J., Widman, M., Lidz, V. & Marlowe, D. (1998). Methadone MT: Its development and effectiveness after 30 years. In J. Inciardi & L. Harrison (Eds.), *Heroin in the Age of Crack-Cocaine* (pp. 60–80). Thousand Oaks, CA: Sage Publications.

Poole, N. & Greaves, L. (Eds.). (2007). *Highs and Lows: Canadian Perspectives on Women and Substance Use.* Toronto: Centre for Addiction and Mental Health. Available: www.camh.net/Publications/CAMH_Publications/highs_lows.html. Accessed March 30, 2009.

Potik, D., Adelson, M. & Schreiber, S. (2007). Drug addiction from a psychodynamic perspective: Methadone maintenance treatment as transitional phenomena. *Psychology and Psychotherapy: Theory, Research and Practice, 80,* 311–325.

Registered Nurses' Association of Ontario (RNAO). (2002). *Toolkit: Implementation of Clinical Practice Guidelines.* Toronto: Author. Available: www.rnao.org/Page.asp?PageID=924&ContentID=823. Accessed March 2009.

Rhodes, G., Saules, K., Helmus, T., Roll, J., BeShears, R., Ledgerwood, D. et al. (2003). Improving on-time counseling attendance in a methadone treatment program: A contingency management approach. *American Journal of Drug and Alcohol Abuse, 29* (4), 759–773.

Ridgely, S. & Willenbring, M. (1992). Application of case management to drug abuse treatment: Overview of models and research issues. In R. Ashery (Ed.), *Progress and Issues in Case Management,* National Institute on Drug Abuse Research Monograph No. 127 (pp. 12–33). Washington, DC: NIDA.

Rollnick, S., Miller, W. & Butler, C. (2008). *Motivational Interviewing in Health Care: Helping Patients Change Behavior (Applications of Motivational Interviewing).* New York: Guilford.

Rosenbaum, M. (1997). The de-medicalization of methadone maintenance. In P. Erickson (Ed.), *Harm Reduction: New Directions for Drug Policies and Programs.* Toronto: University of Toronto Press.

Rosenblum, A., Magura, S., Foote, J., Palij, M., Handelsman, L., Lovejoy, M. et al. (1995). Treatment intensity and reduction in drug use for cocaine dependent methadone patients: A close response relationship. *Journal of Psychoactive Drugs, 27* (2), 151–159.

Rounsaville, B., Weissman, M., Kleber, H. & Wilber, C. (1982). Heterogeneity of psychiatric diagnosis in treated opiate addicts. *Archives of General Psychiatry, 39* (2), 161–166.

Royal College of General Practitioners. (2004). *Guidance for the use of buprenorphine for the treatment of opioid dependence in primary care.* London, UK: Author.

Saxon, A., Wells, E., Fleming C., Jackson, R. & Calsyn, D. (1994). *Pre-treatment characteristics, program philosophy and level of ancillary services as predictors of* MMT *outcome.* Research report presented at annual scientific meeting of the College on Problems of Drug Dependence. Palm Beach, FL: Society for the Study of Addiction to Alcohol and Other Drugs.

Schiff, M., El-Bassel, N., Engstrom, M. & Gilbert, L. (2002). Psychological distress and intimate physical and sexual abuse among women in methadone maintenance treatment programs. *Social Service Review, 76* (2), 302–320.

Schuckit, M. & Hasselbrock, V. (1994). Alcohol dependence and anxiety disorders: What is the relationship? *American Journal of Psychiatry, 151,* 1723–1734.

Scott, J., Gilvarry, E. & Farrell, M. (1998). Managing anxiety and depression in alcohol and drug dependence. *Addictive Behaviors, 23,* 919–931.

Seivewright, N. (2000). *Community Treatment of Drug Misuse: More Than Methadone.* Cambridge, UK: Cambridge University Press.

Sindelar, J., Olmstead, T. & Peirce, J. (2007). Cost-effectiveness of prize-based contingency management in methadone maintenance treatment programs. *Addiction, 102* (9), 1463–1471.

Skinner, W. (Ed.). (2005). *Treating Concurrent Disorders: A Guide for Counsellors.* Toronto: Centre for Addiction and Mental Health.

Statistics Canada. (2006). *Measuring Violence Against Women: Statistical Trends 2006* [catalogue 85-570-x15]. Ottawa: Author. Available: www.statcan.gc.ca/pub/85-570-x/85-570-x2006001 -eng.pdf. Accessed March 30, 2009.

Stevens, A., Radcliffe, P., Sanders, M. & Hunt, N. (2008). Early exit: Estimating and explaining early exit from drug treatment. *Harm Reduction Journal, 5* (13).

Stewart, D., Gossop, M. & Marsden, J. (2004). Increased caseloads in methadone treatment programs: Implications for the delivery of services and retention in treatment. *Journal of Substance Abuse Treatment, 27* (4), 301–306.

Stocco, P., Llacer, J., De Fazio, L., Facy, F., Mariani, E., Legl, T. et al. (2002). *Women and Opiate Addiction: A European Perspective.* Valencia, Spain: Martin Impresores.

Strike, C., Leonard, L., Millison, M., Anstice, S., Berkely, N. & Medd, E. (2006). *Ontario Needle Exchange Programs Best Practice Recommendations.* Toronto: Ontario Needle Exchange Coordinating Committee.

Swiss Society of Addiction Medicine (SSAM). (2007). *Clinical Recommendations for Substitution-Assisted Treatment (SAT) in Opioid Dependence.* Bern, Switzerland: Author.

Telemental Health and Teleaddictions Partnership. (2006). *Project Mawi Wolakomiksultine: Evaluation Report.* Fredericton, NB: Atlantic Evaluation Group and The Quaich.

U.K. Department of Health Scottish Office, Department of Health Welsh Office & Department of Health and Social Services Northern Ireland. (1999). *Drug Misuse and Dependence: Guidelines on Clinical Management.* Colegate, Norwich, UK: Her Majesty's Stationery Office.

Van den Bosch, L. & Verheul, R. (2007). Patients with addiction and personality disorder: Treatment outcomes and clinical implications. *Journal of Current Opinion in Psychiatry, 20,* 67–71.

Verster, A. & Buning, E. (2000). *Methadone Guidelines.* Amsterdam, The Netherlands: Euro-Methwork.

Warj, J., Mattick, R. & Hall, W. (1992). *Key Issues in* MMT. Sydney, Australia: University of New South Wales Press.

Wood, E., Lim, R. & Kerr, T. (2006). Initiation of opiate addiction in a Canadian prison: A case report. *Harm Reduction Journal, 3,* article 11.

Wood, E., Montaner, J., Li, K., Barney, L., Tyndal, M. & Kerr, T. (2007). Rate of methadone use among Aboriginal opioid injection drug users. *Canadian Medical Association Journal, 177* (1), 37–40.

Woody, G., Kane, V., Lewis, K. & Thompson, R. (2007). Premature deaths after discharge from methadone maintenance: A replication. *Journal of Addiction Medicine, 1* (4), 180–185.

Woody, G., McLellan, A., Luborsky, L. & O'Brien, C. (1995). Psychotherapy in community methadone programs: A validation study. *American Journal of Psychiatry, 152* (9), 1302–1308.

Zweben, J.E. (1991). Counseling issues in methadone maintenance treatment. *Journal of Psychoactive Drugs, 23* (2), 177–190.

Zweben, J.E., Clark, H.W. & Smith, D.E. (1994). Traumatic experiences and substance abuse: Mapping the territory. *Journal of Psychoactive Drugs, 26* (4), 327–344.

APPENDIX A: OTHER ISSUES

This appendix offers a brief mention of topics that fall outside the scope of this guide but are related areas in the treatment of opioid dependence likely to be of interest to many of the guide's readers: methadone and chronic pain management, withdrawal management and detoxification as an alternative to MMT, and buprenorphine as an alternative to methadone for use in maintenance treatment.

METHADONE FOR CHRONIC PAIN MANAGEMENT

Pain is a significant clinical issue with psychosocial implications. The interplay between pain issues and opioid dependency is multi-layered and complex. Nevertheless, case managers are in a positive position to support, offer referral services to and contribute to the co-ordination and holistic care of clients with concurrent pain and addiction issues who are receiving methadone treatment (Barry et al., 2008).

The panel proposes that:
- clients who are prescribed methadone for pain and for whom addiction issues are present be offered the same access and approach to case management as clients who are prescribed methadone for dependence alone
- if a client on methadone has significant pain issues, case managers work closely with his or her prescribing physician(s) and with pain management experts to ensure comprehensive care
- case managers receive specific, targeted training on the psychosocial interventions and approaches for case management and counselling for methadone-maintained clients who have both chronic pain and opioid dependency. Of particular importance is the need for case managers to acknowledge clients' concerns that their pain may be perceived as not "real" and to recognize that pain and dependency issues are often complex and interrelated.

WITHDRAWAL MANAGEMENT AND DETOXIFICATION

Not all clients who are dependent on opioids want or need methadone. Physicians are in a position to offer alternatives to methadone, and the guidelines of the CPSO (2005) discuss criteria for assessment for and inclusion in or exclusion from MMT.

The panel encourages:
- case managers to become educated about the risks and benefits of alternatives to methadone and buprenorphine treatments for opioid dependency, as well as about current inclusion and exclusion criteria
- case managers to learn how to support clients who are undergoing time-limited non-methadone-based treatment and/or how to connect them with community resources and supports that will provide them with follow-up care
- physicians to ensure that opioid-dependent clients who receive treatments other than methadone or buprenorphine are assessed for their need for further case management and follow-up, and are referred accordingly.

BUPRENORPHINE TREATMENT

Buprenorphine is emerging in Ontario as an alternative medication for the treatment of opioid dependence. At the time of writing, its use is limited, possibly because social service prescription plans and some private insurance plans do not cover the costs of this medication. However, research about buprenorphine maintenance treatment suggests it has positive and effective treatment outcomes (Connock et al., 2007).

The panel found no definitive evidence to suggest that case management approaches for buprenorphine maintenance treatment are significantly different from those used in the provision of MMT services (Copenhaver et al., 2007; Montoya et al., 2005; Fiellin et al., 2006; Royal College of General Practitioners, 2004; NSW Opioid Treatment Program, 2006).

Further developments in our knowledge of the impact and role of case management and the possibly unique needs of clients receiving buprenorphine treatment are likely.

Therefore, the panel encourages case managers to educate themselves about buprenorphine dispensing and prescribing protocols and treatment efficacy and considerations and to stay abreast of emerging case management issues that are unique to buprenorphine as the body of research grows.

As well, the panel proposes that the recommendations for best practices in case management found in this guide be updated in light of evidence related to case management in buprenorphine treatment as the research emerges.

APPENDIX B: RESOURCES

For more information on camh publications, educational resources and training programs, please visit www.camh.net and follow the links.

The following is a select list of resources from camh and other sources.

FOR CLIENTS AND OTHER MEMBERS OF THE PUBLIC

Methadone Maintenance Treatment: Client Handbook
This guide was developed by camh with the participation of methadone clients across Ontario. It aims to gives clients all the information they need about mmt, including information about length of treatment, side effects, other drugs, counselling, pregnancy, travel, withdrawal and ending treatment. It is written in a clear and easy-to-read style, with many quotes from methadone clients, for those who are thinking about methadone treatment, the new client and the long-term client, and families and friends.

The guide is available in book form or as a downloadable pdf.
- For ordering information, see the copyright page of this guide.
- To download a copy, go to www.camh.net/Care_Treatment/ Resources_clients_families_friends/Methadone_Maintenance_Treatment/ index.html

Concerns or complaints about care
Clients who have already taken reasonable steps to resolve problems directly with their care providers and programs may wish to contact the College of Physicians and Surgeons of Ontario for assistance.

To find out more:
- visit www.cpso.on.ca and follow the "Information about the complaints process" link
- call 416 967-2603 or the Public Advisory department toll-free 1 800 268-7096, extension 603.

ConnexOntario—Drug and Alcohol Registry of Treatment

ConnexOntario Health Services Information is a corporation whose mandate is to improve access to alcohol and drug, gambling and mental health services for the people of Ontario. ConnexOntario operates the Drug and Alcohol Registry of Treatment (DART), the Ontario Problem Gambling Helpline (OPGH) and Mental Health Service Information Ontario (MHSIO), which provide information and referral to services in Ontario.

To find out more:
- visit www.connexontario.ca/index.html
- call 519 439-0174 or toll-free 1 800 565-8603.

FOR EVERYONE INTERESTED IN MMT

Methadone Saves Lives

Methadonesaveslives.ca website is a portal to a comprehensive range of information about opioid dependence and treatment, written accessibly for clients and care providers. It provides the facts that both professionals and people living with opioid drug problems (and their family and friends) need to make informed decisions about MMT.

The site contains information about:
- where to find help and an MMT program
- different types of opioid drugs, including the "Straight Talk" and "Do You Know" pamphlet series
- online tutorials about addiction
- how to order or download copies of CAMH publications, such as *Methadone Maintenance Treatment: Client Handbook* and *Methadone Maintenance Treatment: A Community Planning Guide*
- how to order other educational materials such as the *Prescription for Addiction* DVD and user's guide.

The site also contains information on CAMH's Opiate Dependence Treatment Interprofessional Education Program, which prepares physicians, pharmacists, nurses, counsellors and case managers to provide a comprehensive range of services for people with opioid dependence.
• To explore the site, go to http://methadonesaveslives.ca.

Methadone Maintenance Treatment: A Community Planning Guide
This manual by Mark Erdelyan, Senior Program Consultant, CAMH Windsor, offers guidance to communities on how to educate community members of the benefits of MMT and develop and integrate effective treatment services. It reviews the stages of:
• establishing a community working group
• engaging the community, and
• planning, implementing and evaluating an MMT program.

The resource provides practical suggestions on how to build public support and increase acceptance of those struggling with opioid dependence, through raising community awareness and acceptance of MMT services.
• For more information, search Education and Courses on www.camh.net.

OTHER RESOURCES FOR CASE MANAGERS

Working with injection drug users
For more information on harm reduction, case managers are urged to familiarize themselves with the Ontario Needle Exchange's best practice recommendations on needle exchange programs (Strike et al., 2006).
• The guide is available at www.ohtn.on.ca/compass/Best_Practices_ Report.pdf.

Working with clients who have experienced trauma
An in-depth discussion of trauma is beyond the scope of this guide but readers are encouraged to explore www.trauma-informed.ca, a resource for workers and agencies working with clients with posttraumatic stress disorder. The site contains very practical information written in plain language about trauma-informed approaches.
• For more information, go to www.trauma-informed.ca.

Working with lesbian, bisexual, gay and transgendered clients
CAMH's guide *Asking the Right Questions 2* (ARQ2) will help case managers and other service providers create an environment where all clients feel comfortable talking about their sexual orientation and gender identity.

Lesbian, gay, bisexual, transgendered, transsexual, two-spirit, intersex and queer (LGBTTTIQ) people have specific life factors that relate to substance use and/or mental health problems. These factors include "coming out," gender transition, societal oppression, loss of family support, isolation and the predominance of bars in LGBTTTIQ communities. To provide effective addiction and mental health services, case managers need to be aware of these life factors in clients.

• For more about the *ARQ2* guide or CAMH's one-day *ARQ2* training course, go to www.camh.net/Publications/Resources_for_Professionals/ ARQ2/index.html.

053098746

CPSIA information can be obtained at www.ICGtesting.com
Printed in the USA
LVOW01s2256230514

387191LV00012B/303/P